W9-CCT-962

How to Talk to Your Cat

"Provides an educative and entertaining introduction to the field of animal communication for both adults and young adults."
—*Library Journal*

"An informative and educational blend of personal observation and findings of numerous renowned and lesser-known animal behaviorists."

—*Kirkus Reviews*

*   *   *   *   *   *   *

JEAN CRAIGHEAD GEORGE has shared her home with more than one hundred wild animals and dozens of domestic ones. She is fluent in dogese, catish, and birdic; somewhat less proficient in horse talk, and knows a few words in mink, dolphin, seal, and fox. Her long career as nature writer and member of a famous family of naturalists has put her in touch with the foremost animal behaviorists of our day, as well as with scores of ordinary people who, like her, have learned to talk to the animals by living intimately with them. She divides her time between her home in Chappaqua, New York, and a tent in the wilderness.

Jean Craighead George was awarded the Newbery Medal in 1973 for the most distinguished contribution to American literature for children.

Other Warner Books by Jean Craighead George

HOW TO TALK TO YOUR DOG

How to Talk to Your Cat

Jean Craighead George

Illustrations by the Author

WARNER BOOKS

A Warner Communications Company

This book was formerly published as part of a book entitled
HOW TO TALK TO YOUR ANIMALS.

This book was formerly published as part of a book entitled
HOW TO TALK TO YOUR ANIMALS.

Warner Books Edition
Copyright © 1985 by Jean Craighead George
All rights reserved.

This Warner Books edition is published by arrangement with Harcourt
Brace Jovanovich, Publishers, Orlando, Florida 32887

Warner Books, Inc. 666 Fifth Avenue, New York, NY 10103

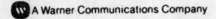 A Warner Communications Company

Printed in the United States of America
First Warner Books Printing: December 1986
10 9 8 7 6

Front cover photograph by Saul White

Library of Congress Cataloging-in-Publication Data

George, Jean Craighead, 1919–
   How to talk to your cat.

   Reprinted from: How to talk to your animals. 1st ed.
San Diego: Harcourt Brace Jovanovich, c1985.
    1. Human-animal communication. 2. Animal communica-
tion. 3. Domestic animals—Behavior. I. George,
Jean Craighead, 1919–   How to talk to your animals.
II. Title.
QL776.G454 1986   636.8'0887   86-15740
ISBN 0-446-39150-6 (U.S.A.) (pbk.)

ATTENTION: SCHOOLS AND CORPORATIONS

Warner books are available at quantity discounts with bulk purchase for educational,
business, or sales promotional use. For information, please write to: Special Sales
Department, Warner Books, 666 Fifth Avenue, New York, NY 10103.

**ARE THERE WARNER BOOKS YOU WANT
BUT CANNOT FIND IN YOUR LOCAL STORES?**

You can get any Warner Books title in print. Simply send title and retail price, plus 50¢ per
order and 50¢ per copy to cover mailing and handling costs for each book desired. New
York State and California residents, add applicable sales tax. Enclose check or money
order—no cash, please—to: Warner Books, PO Box 690, New York, NY 10019. Or send for
our complete catalog of Warner Books.

To Rebecca Jean Pittinger

Contents

How to Talk to Your Cat

Talkier
Than We Knew

A childhood hero of mine was a long-shanked blacksmith with the body of a badger and the eyes of a deer who could talk to the animals. Will Cramer was known as "the man who knows what the animals say." Chickadees clustered around his door; stray dogs came to the gate of his clapboard home as if they had heard through some mysterious grapevine that he would take care of them. Will lived in the valley of the Yellow Breeches Creek in Pennsylvania, down the road from my grandfather's house where my parents, brothers, and I spent our summers. Evenings, my brothers and I often sat on the porch railing of the country store and listened to the farmers talk about crops, the weather, and, now and then, about Will Cramer. "Will listened to a cow bawl today and told Jim Hucklefinger that she wanted to be moved to another stanchion." On another occasion Will heard a dog whine and told his owner, "Your hound wants his collar loosened."

The farmers did not quite believe Will, but did not discredit him either. They were all aware that some kind of communication went on between themselves and their chickens, cows, pigs, horses, cats, and dogs. If it wasn't exactly "talk," it was something akin to it. When the dog barked, they got up and went to see who was approaching the house, and when the cow bawled, they milked her. Communication is, after all, an action by one individual that alters the behavior of another, no matter how humble the creature or how strange the language. A toad excretes a noxious fluid when picked up by bird, beast, or man, that says quite unneatly, "Drop me." Most do.

Will Cramer not only altered his own behavior when the animals spoke to him, he altered theirs by speaking to them in their own language. He asked his dog Nick, who was standing at ease beside him one day, to play by getting down on all fours and spanking the ground with outstretched arms, as dogs do when they are sparking another dog to rough and tumble. He told the cow he wanted her in the meadow by uttering bovine sounds to attract her attention, then stepping in front and walking. In cow language, the animal in the lead is saying, "Follow me."

Anyone watching Will with animals would believe he had some gift not given to other persons, but he told me the year before he died that he just watched what the animals were doing or listened to their vocalizations, then observed what happened next. In other words, Will studied cause and effect, which is how all animal communication functions. A wolf leaves a scent of its presence and social status in its urine at the edge of its territory, and another wolf reads who it is with thoughtful inhalations and either turns away or, recognizing a friend, comes on. "Hello," we say to a person and wait to see the effect of our greeting before going on with the conversation or taking our leave.

Our remarkable communication system—our spoken language, with its infinite combinations of sounds strung together by rules—is so advanced, we believe, compared with nonhuman systems that most of us fail to recognize seemingly simpler dialogues. They are all around us: the cecropia moth calling in chemicals, the spider receiving and sending telegraph messages along a thread, the spreading tail of a peacock speaking of masculinity through a vision of beauty, the wolves keeping their space around them by howling in concert. The odors, poses, movements, displays, and the clicks, hisses, chirps, and bellows are communications. Animals, including us, speak in the four media of scent, touch, sight, and sound. Some messages use but one medium, some all four, but all media, all messages, are the self reaching out to be known by others.

Anyone with even the slightest acquaintance with animals recognizes a kitten's mew as a plea and a dog's bark as a warning. But they are only the tip of the iceberg. Animal communication has turned out to be far more complex than we had guessed until recently.

1920 was a landmark year in our awakening to the true meaning of the prettiest of all animal sounds in nature. That year British businessman Elliot Howard published his discovery that a bird's song is not the outburst of joy we in our innocence had supposed it to be, but a rather businesslike announcement specifically addressed to others of its kind. Birds sing to announce property lines, advertise for a mate, and proclaim ownership of a good habitat for the rearing and feeding of young.

Howard spent years wandering his estate, observing and charting the behavior of resident songbirds. Gradually his notes and diagrams took shape. A certain male bird was always in the same area, he sang from the same bushes and trees, and, no matter how long Howard pressed him, he never left that piece of land. Like himself, the bird had territory, and like himself, he defended it, not with words, laws, and guns, but with song. The seemingly pleasant little bird was threatening his neighbor with, "Keep off my property."

Once Howard recognized this, everyone saw it—and with a deep sense of shock, not so much because birdsong was tough talk, but because it took so many millennia for intelligent mankind to recognize something so obvious.

The discovery of territorial behavior in birds hatched a host of scientific disciplines: ethology, sociobiology, animal behaviorism, cognitive ethology—a potpourri of names for fields in which men and women have put aside the study of conventional physical zoology to observe the thinking, communications, and social behavior of nonhuman animals. Now six decades of their observations have caused a flip-flop in our thinking. We can no longer speak of "dumb" animals. Most natural scientists believe today that the birds and beasts are not automatons, performing by instinct without thought or feeling, but creatures of intelligence and sensitivity that communicate in many ingenious ways. Will Cramer was right: the animals do talk, not only to each other but to us if we listen.

"Talk" and "listen" are impoverished words to use to mean communication; perhaps our reliance on speech explains why we spent so long noticing so little animal palaver. For instance, the oldest, and still most fundamental, medium of communication is chemicals. We are aware of molecule messages as the very few tastes and relatively strong odors we can discern. We consciously use sweets and perfumes in courting. But that's nothing compared with the chemical languages we are not aware of. Every cell of our body is in constant communication through the chemicals called hormones and neurotransmitters. One cell emits molecules of insulin, and another, receiving the word, knows to take up sugar from the bloodstream. Chemical language is most likely all life's mother tongue, for bacteria, from their position on the lowest rung of the phylogenetic ladder, speak in insulin and estrogen. Even plants talk chemically. The alder tree when attacked by insects sends out a chemical vapor that "tells" other nearby alders that insects are attacking. They respond by depleting their leaves of nutrients and loading them with insect-killing toxins. Bacteria speak through chemicals that keep them together where there is food and warmth and bring them together for rare matings.

Scientists are only beginning to unravel chemical communication, but they are sure the lexicon includes the most essential distinction: self and other. Bacteria string along only with their own kind, each joining with others most like itself. On the other hand, a bacterium couples for sexual purposes only with an individual of its own kind that is not identical to itself. The first message might therefore be translated as "I am I," an announcement of species and individual self. Trading such messages, some organisms can apparently gauge their relatedness.

Andy Blaustein, at Oregon State University, recently demonstrated in laboratory tests that pollywogs recognize kin. A pollywog raised separately from its brothers and sisters, and then introduced to them and to unrelated pollywogs of the same species, chose to pal around with its own family.

We ourselves do not seem able to sniff out our degree of kinship, at least we are not aware of it, but apparently we give off a family smell. Nele, a great hairy dog belonging to my friend Sara Stein and very much a part of her family, ran toward a strange man who had parked in the driveway, tasting the air with her nose. Sara was surprised that the dog not only failed to bark at the stranger but bounded up to him in joyful greeting, tail wagging. She looked closer. The man was not a stranger but her cousin, a cousin that Nele had never met but who apparently reeked of relative.

Although our chemical reception is poor compared with a dog's, we do receive and react to some odors, often unconsciously. The smell of a lover lingering on clothes when the lover is away fills us with longing, and the scent of a baby's head elicits tenderness. We no doubt send out odors that announce our sex, but our discernment is nearly subliminal, so we heighten the difference with "feminine" perfume or "masculine" shaving lotion. Few other animals need that hype. Invisible, silent, and unnoticed as these chemicals are to us, our animals easily sniff them out.

A pet red fox I raised had been injured by a man when she was taken from her family den, and ever after she bit or ran from all men. Women she loved, and said so by leaping softly into their lap and draping herself affectionately over their shoulders. It was important to her that she made no mistake, and I soon realized by her reaction of fear even toward objects that men had touched that the red fox could discern maleness and femaleness in the human species far faster and more accurately than I, using my own cultural clues to sex—clothing, voice, and hair. While I often ponder or make mistakes through my eyes and ears, the red fox's nose was instantly correct.

Chemical communication is probably behind dogs' almost eerie ability to read our moods and feelings. While camping with me and my son one summer my son's friend Seaver Jones thought he heard a grizzly bear snapping sticks as it came toward our camp. There was no bear, but Seaver's fear was so great that Jake, his dog, smelled it and raised the hair on his back. Finding nothing himself to fear on the wind, Jake licked Seaver's face and went back to sleep.

Seaver, of course, had no difficulty interpreting Jake's affectionate face lick.

Touch speaks forcefully and intimately, especially among mammals, whose strokes, pats, nibbles, licks, and kisses share a common heritage of motherly love. Mammal mothers and babies literally keep in touch, and so do lovers. But even turtles touch. Last June I watched a male box turtle in my woods approach a female at sundown and after a few surprisingly agile maneuvers for a rock-hard creature, climb upon her back and caress her with loving taps of his lower bony carapace. His touch spoke clearly. She mated with him.

We humans speak of love as we caress, of fear as we cling, of restraint as we grip, and of aggression as we shove. We evoke laughter by tickling. We also send messages to our animals through touch, conveying thoughts that perhaps we do not consciously realize we are saying. The pat on the head we give our animals is a substitute for "Blessings on you, little man," a condescending but reassuring gesture that says, "Remain a child. I'll take care of you."

And our animals speak back to us through touch, although they are not always saying exactly what we think they are. Cats' rubbing and dogs' licking are certainly affectionate statements, but the cat rubs against us to claim us as its beloved possession, and the dog licks us to express its lovingly subordinate position.

I go to the garden to touch talk with a spider, the wizard of tactile communication. I pull very gently on its web; the owner, a female spider, pulls back on the thread. Through her telegraph system she asks, "Who are you?" I could be a male spider or an insect to eat. I pull again, and this time I say with my clumsiness, "Human being." She replies that she knows I am a predator by running up another thread and hiding.

I try other things on her. I shake the web with a slim stalk of grass, hoping to say, "Food," then I sprinkle water to say, "The dew of dawn." I wait for her reply. She does not come out. I toss a katydid in her web, and this time she answers me by dashing out and killing it. I learn her definitions of the insects, for she reacts differently to grasshoppers and gnats, enshrouding each with a defining silk that virtually bears the insect's name. A thick band thrown from a distance is "bee," a broad swath wrapped at close quarters while her feet spin the prey reads "grasshopper," a single thread says "gnat."

To a spider, touch brings messages from a distance along the far-flung web of her communication system. Were a male spider to court her—by drumming his love tattoo from a safe distance before approaching his dangerous bride—she would receive the message in time to avoid harming him. But touch ordinarily requires actual contact, and smell, too, is commonly an intimate communication. The prime long-distance sense in higher land animals is vision. We see and interpret before we encounter. Visual signals, such as a stallion's proud posing on the rim of a distant hill, can be sent over greater distances than animal sound—miles compared to half a mile for the loudest noisemaker, the cicada.

Strangely, until very recently we remained unaware of visual signals of our own more subtle than a wave or a smile. Now, with our knowledge of "body language," we are in a better position to appreciate the expressive faces, poses, and gestures of other animals. Even bodily proportions speak. The proportions of kittens and puppies elicit a parenting response in us, and we say, "Aaaaw," and pick them up. What is talking to us are the large head and eyes, the small body, and short, plump limbs. "I am cute. I am helpless, hold me, care for me," the baby proportions cry out. We are not taught the message of proportions; it comes from deep in our nonintellectual being, down with loving and needing.

Our animals also reply to babyish proportions with parental behavior, even when the baby is another species. Our bluetick hound, Delilah, had such a response to my son Luke when he was a baby. She licked and encircled him and leaped into his crib to curl warmly beside him when I was in another room. She did not do this to Luke's six-year-old sister or four-year-old brother or to me. That's baby power for you.

Adults display their power by posture, and these visual signals, too, are well-nigh universal. The signal is given by making oneself appear big. The wolf says "I am leader of the pack" by holding his head higher than the others. The gull chief throws out his chest and stretches his neck above his kin to announce his dominance. The male songbird puffs up his feathers to speak of his importance and aggressiveness. Kings, queens, and presidents are taught to carry themselves erect. Military officers thrust out their chests like pigeons to say the same thing—"I am dominant and powerful."

The opposite message—one that indicates a low position on the social ladder or an acknowledgment of inferiority in an encounter—is given by making oneself appear small or childlike. The wolf and dog roll over puppylike on their backs in deference, the low-order gull pulls in its neck and crouches, and the humble servant bows to royalty. These postures are extremes and therefore are easy to recognize.

But there are as well an infinite number of other communicative poses, including those of the face, that amplify, dampen, and even contradict "outspoken" messages. Many of our facial expressions—from smiles to frowns—are congruent with what we are saying: when a dear friend says, "I am so happy to see you," the broad smile amplifies the spoken message. We are aware that this is not always so. Even children pick up an insincere smile, despite its being coupled with the words "What an adorable child!" By filming people in stressful situations, such as getting fired, psychologists in California have compiled a "dictionary" of facial messages that contradict spoken statements. Written on these faces are such messages as "masked anger," "overly polite," and "resigned compliance." Facial expressions speak truer than words.

Few other animals have such well-developed—or even as many—facial muscles as we, so a horse's or cat's face seems rather blank to us. To understand what they are saying, we have to learn to read ears, whiskers, the pupils of the eye, and the glint of teeth. They, too, can modify a voiced message. A dog growling with ears pricked is quite sincere in its threat to bite. A dog growling with ears lowered is as frightened as it is annoyed.

Light is another form of visual communication in the nonhuman world, and none uses it so beautifully as the firefly. I grew up in firefly country. When I asked my grandfather why they had lights, he answered, "Because lights are lovely. That's reason enough," and I accepted that. In the late 1950s a persistent firefly observer discovered something that changed the summer night for me. "The lights are a language," he told me one evening. "A simple code. When flashed, the signal is 'Yes'; when off, it means 'No.' He pointed to the lights above the meadow.

"The fireflies that are blinking and climbing upward are males advertising their sex, which species they are, and their sexual readiness to the females in the grass."

Now as I walk along a stream at dusk, I see loveliness and much more. I see the drama of firefly love. A male glows at the top of an ironweed, lifts his hard outer wings, vibrates his gossamer underwings, and takes off. He climbs, flashing his lamp at a leisurely beat as he courts the females first with slow strokes, then faster and faster. They watch from below. When he reaches the tops of the trees, his call comes even more urgently; the night is passing. A female at the base of a clump of foxtail grass is finally aroused. Her light goes on— "Yes." The male fastens his many-faceted eyes on her and descends. He, too, is ready. His light says, "Yes."

The lamp in the grass goes out—"No." Did another male find her and turn off her light? The downward-gliding male still flashes his bold visual cries and is answered by another light in the grass. He descends, flying past a male who at that instant is caught by a bat, nipped, and crushed with his light on. He falls, his continuous glow becoming a statement of death. It is not a communication, for no firefly upon seeing it changes its behavior. All continue to shine and signal. The glowing body falls to earth like a star and goes out. "No."

The male I am watching drifts into the meadow grass. The "No" female of the foxtail lights up again—"Yes." He touches down on her grass blade.

Both lights go out. The firefly embrace is invisible to bat, frog, skunk, and me, and a conversation in lights is over.

As lovely as this conversation is, to most people the ultimate in visual communication is the peacock. Every pattern and color, from the iridescent head, chest, neck, and golden coverts to the spreading tail and wings, says, "Choose me. I'm beautiful." The peacock's beauty is a result of what is called sexual selection. The peahens have created this wondrous creature over the eons by selecting the most beautiful male to be father of their offspring. And because of their eye, we have among us the super star of visual talk.

Honeybees employ dance to communicate visually with their sisters. Sociobiologist Edward O. Wilson compares their language to our own because they can, like us, speak in symbols. Through a dance one bee passes on to another information removed in time and space.

A forager bee returning to the hive after finding a good source of nectar and pollen alights on a hive wall and runs a figure eight until she gathers her sisters around her. As she dances she puts the emphasis on the *straight-line run* down the middle of the figure by vibrating her body. Were she dancing on a flat surface, the straight-line run would point directly to the flowers. But the hive wall is vertical, so the bee, in effect, pins the map up on the wall. Just as we might use the compass points to describe direction—twenty degrees east of north—she uses the present position of the sun—twenty degrees to the right of the sun. But the hive is dark, so, by convention, she uses "up" to indicate the sun's position. We use a similar convention: north is "up" on our maps.

The distance to the flowers is calculated and translated into time. In one species of honeybee, a run of one second duration indicates the food is five hundred meters away. A two-second run states that the nectar is two kilometers from the hive. During the dance the sister bees call upon other communication systems. They touch the dancer to discern the vigor of her waggling, an indication of how promising she considers her find. The smell and taste of the pollen and nectar on the dancer tell them what flowers they will be looking for. Once briefed, they take off; and the majority arrive dead on target—which I couldn't do by following verbal directions.

Communications so unlike our own as the bee's dance have taken researchers untold hours of observation and experiment to decipher. They are not languages that Will Cramer, blessed as he was with intuition, could have translated. He, like most of us, was more at home with sounds.

As an admirer of animal sonance, I seek out, in the early summer, the most famous theater for croaks, growls, squawks, songs, trills, pipes, and whistles—the swamp. Up from the water surface, out of the reeds, and over the floating plants soars the full choir of animal voices. Insects, amphibians, reptiles, birds, and mammals speak with such volume that I am tempted to add a human song to the glorious clangor. One spring night while camping in the Okefenokee Swamp of Georgia, I heard between sundown and sunup barred owls hooting, alligators bellowing, a wildcat caterwauling, raccoons growling, twenty-two species of frogs piping, and several hundred species of insects buzzing, clicking, whining, and humming. In the dawn light, the shriek of the wood ibis, the carol of the vireo, the rasp of the pileated woodpecker were added, one voice upon another, hundreds of species strong. It was a night and dawn of expressive doings, and my great pleasure was that I could translate a few of their phrases because of the new knowledge in animal communications.

That new knowledge is, however, minuscule. We are on one side of a great abyss that separates human from animal language, and the distance often seems uncrossable. How can we really know what is going through a dog's mind when it wags its tail? We can never get inside its brain. But we cannot get inside each other's minds either. How do I know you see the color green as I see green? What is important is that the dog sees something and is wagging its tail. What it is that makes the dog happy is where we should be looking. As it happens, dogs wag their tails only to living objects—butterflies or people—but never to anything inanimate or dead, not even to a bone. That says something about dogs, even if we can't come up with an exact translation for what they are trying to convey to a butterfly. There is a why to smell, touch, sight, and sound signals, and the why is to be found, as Will Cramer saw, in what happens next. When dogs wag their tails to one another, they then approach in a friendly manner.

So we know that friendliness spells happiness to dogs. Perhaps they invite butterflies to play across an abyss much greater than the one that separates our two mammalian species— one that never will be bridged.

When I read who on this earth was the first speaker to have organs specifically designed to make noise, I felt as if someone had thrown a rope across even that impossible abyss for me. The first voice was so simple and so sensible. It was uttered by an insect, a grasshopper, a fragment of which lies trapped in a fossil 200 million years old. The grasshopper had sound-making files on its wings almost like those of the modern grasshopper. Back in that mist of time, the file owner rubbed his wings together and vibrated the air. The ripple reached a receptor on another of his kind, and she followed the sound to its source. They mated. The first noisemaker needed never again to waste time and energy running around looking for a mate.

To become aware of the languages other species speak is thrilling, but to exchange conversations in these lexicons with another species is the quintessential effort. We all wish we could hold a discourse with our animals, if only to know how they like us. A few people manage to communicate across the abyss with little effort: the rare Will Cramers, a handful of scientists. But there are universal messages that wing across the gap when we least expect it. My brother, John, had a pet coyote named Crooner many years ago in Wyoming. The pup moved on the fringes of John's family life but was never really a part of it. He would come in to play, request food and affection from time to time, and then vanish into his own world in the sagebrush. One day while John was nailing shingles on the roof of his house, he saw his two-year-old son tumble into the irrigation ditch. He still does not know if he yelled or simply scrambled frantically to get off the roof, but the coyote received a distress message from him, appeared like a white knight, and pulled Derek out of the water.

"Danger to the young," he must have conveyed, and the coyote understood it.

Will Cramer never opened a book on animal behavior or took a course in dog obedience, yet he talked to the animals, according to his own analysis, by listening for those expressions we all have in common and conversing on those subjects.

One day I asked Will to tell me how I could let his cat know I wanted to be her friend. He demonstrated by making soft squeaky noises with his lips and holding out his hand. I made soft squeaky noises and held out my hand—and was swatted.

"Too much eye," Will said. "To ask a cat to be a friend, you have to mostly look away." Then he added, "Besides, you smell wrong. The cat smells that you think people are the only critters who can talk."

And he was right. An inside voice from my background in a scientific family was pulling, saying, "Don't anthropomorphize. Don't attribute human thoughts and emotions to animals."

Years later, after raising 173 wild and 50 domestic pets, I still felt that pull, although I had learned to peep like a quail and make hand signals to our mink to invite her to leap and tumble on the back of the couch. Despite such enormous triumphs, my human viewpoint prevailed—only people can truly converse.

It was not until I read a scientific paper on the language of the wolves by the esteemed animal behaviorist Rudolf Schenkel of Switzerland that I believed there were other languages and perfectly brilliant conversations going on on the other side of the abyss. Wolves talk among themselves, Schenkel observed, with eyes, postures, scents, body contact, mood, and voice. And we can use the same signals to talk to wolves.

A few phone calls to wolf enthusiasts informed me that wolf talk and human talk was being exchanged at the Naval Arctic Research Lab in Barrow, Alaska, on the North Slope where the Arctic Ocean laps the land. I approached a national magazine, took on the assignment to "talk to a wolf," packed up, and flew with my youngest son, Luke, to the Top of the World. In that Arctic wildland I interviewed the authorities on wolf behavior and observed the wolves for many long twenty-four-hours-of-daylight days, listening for the only thing I understood at the time—the sounds of whimpers, howls, sniffs, and barks. After practicing the sounds, I felt I was ready to make the crossing of the abyss. I selected a beautiful female I called Silver. She was almost white, her eyes were gold and serene, her disposition, despite her confinement in a large enclosure, was sweet. In broken wolfese, I whimpered my affection and asked her to be my friend.

She ignored me.

"Your pose is wrong," wolf-language expert Dr. Michael Fox said. "Say it with your body." I stood more confidently and moved with more dignity. Still no response. Fox assumed a kingly attitude. I copied his posture and lifted my head with authority, but my whimpers and poses still brought no response from Silver. I was not getting through. There was no change in her behavior. She walked past me as if I were less than a pebble on the tundra.

The day before I was to leave Barrow, I went back to my notes and read something I had skimmed over. The wolf father leads the pack on the hunt, the mother attends to the pups, and baby-sitters and the puppies mock fight, tumble, and play games. The wolf family is very much like the human family; within it conflicts arise and arguments are settled, jobs are assigned and done.

A feeling of similarity replaced my feeling of strangeness. Silver and I had much in common. We were both parents, females; we both watched and disciplined our young, taught them safety rules, encouraged their play, and stopped their aggressions. We had common ground on which to meet and talk. I put away my notebook and went back to the animal lab.

When I approached Silver's enclosure on this last visit and whimpered to her, she hesitated and . . . passed me by.

But as I turned to leave, Silver stopped in her tracks, then galloped back to me. She smiled. Wolves pull back their lips and smile just as we pull back our lips and smile, and for the same reasons. They are pleased, or they like you.

With that smile she let me in. I was not a pebble on the tundra. I was in her consciousness. Having admitted me, she continued the conversation. She wagged her tail, looked me in the eye, and whimpered in a high thin voice, "Uummum," the wolf plea for friendship.

I whimpered, "Uummum." Silver wagged her tail enthusiastically, spanked the ground with her forepaws, and asked me to play. I, at long last, was talking to a wolf.

I did not do anything differently that last meeting with Silver, but I felt differently. I had drawn on our likenesses, not our differences, and, in doing so, I had come down from the pedestal that human beings put themselves on. As Will Cramer might have said, I "smelled right."

The conversations that await us as we learn to reach across the abyss are no doubt full of surprises. One man, Dr. George Archibald, founder of the International Crane Foundation, Baraboo, Wisconsin, must know this better than anyone. He heads an institution dedicated to saving from extinction the stately cranes, among them the whooping crane. Archibald has studied crane communications and their behavior so thoroughly that he can not only share the universal meeting ground with them but *really* talk and get them to answer.

A female whooping crane named Tex, one of the last 150, was given to Archibald by the San Diego Zoo. The bird was imprinted on people; that is, she had been raised from an egg by humans, and she thought she was human, too. When she matured, she fell in love with Archibald.

At five years, when she was of breeding age, she would not mate with her own kind for love of Archibald, and so she was artificially inseminated.

It did not take. Tex was unable to ovulate without the stimulation of courtship. But she, like others raised in captivity, would not tolerate the attention of a bird of her species.

Archibald saw a possibility in his relationship with Tex and decided to try his luck.

He would walk slowly into her outdoor enclosure and begin to speak to her of love in her own language. When she flapped her wings—the equivalent of a wink from a lady in our own body language—he would flap his preposterous and awkward arms. As clumsy as this suitor was, she encouraged him because she loved him and he was talking crane talk. She would float into the air and drop back to earth. He would jump and come down. He would utter strange cries in response to hers and spend as much time as he could spare walking and waltzing with Tex. She was inseminated and laid an egg. But the egg was not fertile. Tex had not reached the climax of crane courtship, and without achieving this, her eggs could not be fertilized.

The following breeding season Archibald took time off from his travels and duties and devoted the day to Tex from sunrise to sunset. They met in the morning and flapped arms and wings. They leaped lightly over the grass and jumped into the air, Archibald stretching his neck in imitation of Tex's stretch. They walked together, gathered worms together, and finally built a nest of grass and corncobs together. One morning when Tex danced with more excitement than Archibald had seen before, she was artificially inseminated. It took. A fertile egg was laid on May 3, 1982. The whooping crane Gee Whizz was hatched on June 3.

In the following chapters you will learn the history, social behavior, and language of cats—animals that touch our lives very closely.

"Animal talk is on the other side of words," Will Cramer once told me as he explained his uncanny communication with his dog Nick. "He watches my eyes to know what I am thinking; I watch his." But Archibald could not have courted a crane without studying its biology and learning the meanings of its whoops, leaps, and flaps.

So on the one hand, my guide will be the intuition of pet owners who, by their experience, just know how to talk to animals, without knowing exactly how or why what they do works.

On the other hand, my guide will be the scientists who have unraveled a few of the mysterious threads of animal communication through careful and objective research.

For those who need more than Will Cramer and the scientists to make them believe that they, too, can cross the abyss, may I say that if alder trees can communicate with alder trees, why not dogs with dogs, and cats with cats?

And for those who accept this but doubt that cats can talk to people and people to cats, let me mention that creosote bushes can communicate with weed and flower seeds in the soil beneath them—and tell them chemically not to grow.

When I learned that, I went out and talked to everything.

The Cat

The cat Danny was not fed for the two days that my friend Joan Gordon was delayed out of town. He had a door through which he could come and go to his hunting grounds, where he often caught mice, and Joan was not overly concerned about him. He was, after all, a cat, capable and independent, the perfect predator. Joan had left him on his own before.

As she came up the path to the house, she smiled to hear Danny meowing his chirruping welcome. Eagerly she opened the door.

"Hello, Danny, old fellow. I'm glad to see you. Hello." The hefty, ruddy tabby cat looked right at her face and chirruped again. His fur was pressed lightly to his body, his whiskers were bowed forward, his pupils were dilated with pleasure, his tail was held straight up like a flag pole, and he danced on his toes: an altogether exuberant greeting, perhaps best translated as "Hello, hello, hello, hello."

But something amiss caught Joan's attention. A kitchen

chair had been knocked over, by Danny no doubt, and one leg had jammed his door closed. The cat had not eaten after all.

With great concern Joan dropped her coat and suitcase, opened a can of food, and put it on the floor.

But Danny did not eat.

Hungry as he must have been, he ran to Joan and repeated the redundant greeting. Next he rubbed Joan's ankles with his head, then with his flank, and then snaked his tail over her shins, all the while purring. He arched his back toward her hand, asking to be petted. She obliged and then again urged food on him.

Danny ignored the food and went on with his cat talk. He rose on his hind legs and arched his shoulders and neck toward Joan's hand, asking more forcefully this time to be petted again. When Joan stroked him, he purred like a motorcycle. Finally Danny turned to the food, only to take one bite and return to repeat the entire exuberant, sensual, deeply felt, and minutes-long "Welcome-home" routine again.

Joan called me that night, incredulous. Danny, she now knew, put her before a can of food.

A TALK WITH AN UNEXPECTED GUEST

It is quite typical of cats to greet their human friends before eating—even after a prolonged fast. Some insist on socializing as a prelude to any meal. Skitters, the plume-tailed coon cat of my doctor's wife, will not touch the food Marilyn has put down each morning until he has sniffed her and rubbed her with his flanks. He arches, asking to be stroked. Marilyn caresses him, and Skitters then will take a bite, but still he will not finish his food until she has picked him up and performed the ultimate in cat greetings—best described as head bumping.

Cats recognize humans, faces and voices, and even their cars. One or two minutes before Joan pulls into her driveway, Danny hears her car approaching many blocks away and stations himself at the door to greet her. Not only do cats actively seek the affection of their "owner," they tolerate a

Head bumping

good deal of abuse from other members of their family. Children who, for some reason, are wont to pick up a kitty by the middle, causing it to dangle head down, are less often scratched than they deserve, and some remarkably pacific cats allow themselves to be dressed in baby clothes and pushed in a pram. Not a few cats consider that the only appropriate sleeping arrangement is to be cuddled in bed with their human. Paul Leyhausen, a German scientist who studied house cats for twenty years in great thoroughness and detail, concluded in no uncertain terms that "the domestic cat can have a warm and loving relationship with human beings."

Yet the friendship between humans and cats is something that scientists would not have predicted and that they find difficult to explain. Unlike dogs, which are social animals and respond to our family as they respond to their own, cats are loners. They scorn other cats, aggressively keeping them at a distance or passively avoiding meetings whenever possible. They hunt by themselves.

Cats are designed for a pounce-from-ambush hunting strategy. "Wild" colors and patterns, still seen in the tawny shades of the domesticated Abyssinian breed and the familiar red- or gray-striped tabbies, are camouflage that can render the immobile cat invisible as it silently awaits its prey. The feline backbone is exceptionally limber; it has five more sacral vertebrae than the human backbone, enabling cats to flex, stretch, and twist a good 180 degrees. Although not cut out for marathons, cats in full stride can cover four times the length of their body at each leap, change direction in midair, and pounce upon their prey with deadly speed and agility.

Their eyes are larger than any other carnivore's in relation to their head size, a feature that attracts people because it gives them a babylike and innocent look. Their excellent sight is surpassed only by their exquisite sense of smell and by hearing that is deftly tuned to the rustling sounds of prey in dry grass or leaves and the ultrasonic squeaks of mice. Cats are the most successful of the mammal predators, catching their quarry 50 percent of the time as compared with wolves' 20 percent, and a good mouser of the pussycat sort does even better.

Wild kittens, like the young of most mammals, are friendly and trusting of humans. But the wild cats of the world cannot form reliably warm relationships with people that last into adulthood. They can be "tamed," even trained, as circus animals, for instance; they cannot be relieved of an inherent fear of man. What friendliness can be achieved by an individual cat is not carried on into the next generation. A British zoologist raised from kittens two wild Egyptian, or Kaffir, cats, which are considered to be the progenitors of the domestic cat. They were tame and pleasant creatures, but their offspring were as wary of humans as if they had grown up in the wild. They ran from people, stole food from the table, and when smacked for doing so, would not jump down as do domestic cats but would stand their ground, lay back their ears, spit, bare their teeth, and try to bite.

Dogs can be bred back to wolves or coyotes and still remain domestic animals. That also is not reliably so in cats. Naturalist Frances Pitt of England reported that the offspring of a mating between the Kaffir's wild European relative and a domestic cat had inherited the disposition of the wild cat. They were nervous and bad tempered, attacked Pitt's geese, and ran off to the woods. She had to lock them up because they could not be trusted.

So why is it that house cats live so well with people?

Geneticists offer an explanation: Domestication was enabled by a genetic change, but a very subtle and tenuous one. Although the domestic cat, *Felis catus,* resembles its wild counterpart, *Felis sylvestris,* in almost every other respect, one thing is different: It fails to develop wariness toward people in adulthood.

The change was not something accomplished by people who captured, tamed, and bred wild cats to a more relaxed disposition, but people did have something to do with it. Sometime before about seven thousand years ago, it seems likely, wild Kaffir cats in North Africa and the Middle East began to take advantage of human civilizations then developing along the Nile and other rivers. The people there were forming civilizations centering on the growing and storing of grain. This massive collection of seeds permitted mice to thrive on a scale that no wild rodent had before enjoyed and that no rodent predator had before encountered. The wild cats moved in close to this bonanza. These oddball cats that could tolerate people lived well and passed on this boldness to their offspring. So one could say that while people provided the opportunity, cats pretty much domesticated themselves. Their evolutionary "guess" happened to be correct, for in fact we did not do battle with cats but welcomed their predations on destructive rodents. Consequently, this charming beast—which does not defer to a leader as dogs do, is not a follower like horses, sheep, and cattle, and is not gregarious like chickens and ducks—found us to be pleasant enough, and our supply of rodents rich enough, to move intimately into our lives by perhaps 4000 B.C. in Egypt. Cat remains from that time show the first signs that some were being purposefully bred, perhaps as pets.

The human-tolerant cat seems to have lived within our communities for more than a millennium before we took historical note of its presence or expressed our admiration for its talents and beauty. But by 2500 B.C. the cat's likeness was being drawn on Egyptian papyrus, painted on frescoes, shaped in silver and gold, sculptured in ivory, and carved out of precious gems.

Around 2000 B.C. the cat was elevated to the status of a goddess—Bast, symbol of grace, fertility, and femininity. So revered was this animal that it became a felony to kill it. Bodies of cats were mummified with the reverence and care accorded a pharaoh; some were buried in gold caskets. They must have been, by then, beloved pets. Yet most were still physically identical to Kaffir cats, *Felis sylvestris,* not *Felis catus.* Mummified cats found in the tombs of pharaohs of 2000 B.C. are Kaffir cats, according to zoologists of the London Museum of Natural History, and all but three of the 300,000 mummified cats entombed around 1800 B.C. at the village of Bani Hasan, are also Kaffirs. Even by 1350 B.C., when Queen Nefertiti, the beauty of antiquity, painted her eyes in the likeness of cats' eyes, the pattern she chose to honor resembles the facial markings of the Kaffir.

Ultimately the domestic cat was distinguished from its wilder ancestors by a slightly altered body, especially by shorter legs and a narrower skull, but the differences are not nearly so dramatic as are those between domestic dogs and their canid ancestors.

Exportation of the cat from Egypt was forbidden during the years of its deification, so the domestic cat did not appear elsewhere until around 1000 A.D., when it was brought to China. Several centuries later, cats spread to Japan and Europe, possibly making their way to these countries smuggled aboard the ships of the globe-traveling Phoenicians, who gave no credence to the Egyptian belief in feline sacredness. Once scattered, these pleasant cats mated with various closely related wild cats of Europe and Asia, whose genes are now also represented in the many modern breeds. Although there are at least thirty breeds of cats today, most are not unlike the original. Black (melanistic) fur, white (albinistic) fur, and fur with Siamese coloration are the result of mutations, as are the tailless rear end of the Manx and coats of odd textures, such as the curly coat of the rex.

In Europe during the Middle Ages the cat was shunned as a symbol of paganism. It was considered an animal of the devil and killed in great numbers. Only a hint of that dread still lingers in superstitions and Halloween traditions, but the cat remains the most controversial of all domestic animals. There are cat lovers, and cat haters, and few in-betweeners.

The fact is that the genetic change that launched cats toward domesticity left them surprisingly unchanged. House cats have retained a good measure of wildness; some people like that, and some people do not. Their fights are passionate, their pleasures sensuous; yet their killing is a model of cool precision, and they cannot hide a fundamental aloofness that stems from their solitary way of life.

Cats can and do live on their own without help from people. Feral cats and kittens raised in woods, parks, or city streets spit and press back their ears like their wild brethren when they meet up with people. Even pet cats are not totally dependent upon us, and we have not much altered their appearance or behavior with breeding. Their hunting skills have not changed. Their favored prey is mice and rats. They still don't care much for the company of other cats. After all these millennia, the cat remains an unexpected guest, who can be convinced to stay only by nurturing its subtle failure of wariness and by courting it on its own wild terms. Some people welcome the challenge. Others close the door in its face.

ON BEING A FAVORED PLACE

Whereas a dog joins in with us, a cat moves in. Both kittens and old cats take over the whole environment, which includes mice in the woodwork, pathways through the yard, food in a dish, sunning spots, lookout posts, hideouts, resting places, and, as it happens, humans.

Upon moving in, the cat brings with it from the wilds the cat concept of home. Immediately it cases the area and, whether it is a newly weaned baby or an adopted adult, sets up a uniquely catlike kind of territory divided into a central *first-order home* and a surrounding *second-order* area. The first-order home may correspond to your home, or to only part of it, or to home plus yard. The second-order home corresponds roughly to our idea of neighborhood. What makes the central and peripheral areas unlike wolf or human territory is that the cat does not seem to consider them whole, inviolable spaces. Rather, your home to your cat is a number

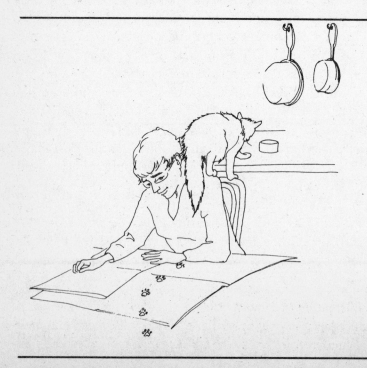

of regularly visited localities—places for resting, sunbathing, keeping watch, and eating. These are connected by an elaborate network of pathways. Although the cat adheres to the paths, it knows all the territory in between and scrutinizes it daily. But the route and the favorite places it connects are the thing. My friend Sara Stein's huge black-and-white cat, William, meows to clear her off his path to his morning sunbathing stop but does not bother with formalities on his route to his breakfast place, which is over the kitchen table and down. If she is sitting there, it is onto her shoulder and down her back.

After breakfast, William retraces that path to his first rest stop, Sara's lap. Although he purrs and enjoys being petted, it is the place that matters. If Sara is concentrating on the newspaper and not moving to acknowledge his presence, William "arranges" her arm to suit by pulling it over with both front paws. Then he lays his head down upon it. He snoozes, purring just as loudly as he would if he were being lavishly petted. He is happiest, Sara has learned by making mistakes, when his "place" does not cross her legs, shift her position, or turn the pages of the paper.

Although we make laps all the time, it is your cat's decision as to when to use them. You can't dictate to a cat. My daughter Twig had a charming tortoiseshell female named Trinket. She lived and raised her annual litter of kittens with us for thirteen years. Yet whenever I wanted Trinket in my lap, she would not stay more than a moment. When she decided it was lap time, I could not get rid of her.

Sara says William's routine was established when he was a tiny kitten, one of a litter raised in her home. Cats are very much creatures of habit who expect their environment to produce laps, patches of sunlight, and bowls of food on schedule. Making your habits and your person fit your cat's expectations are matters of noticing its daily appointment calendar and of seeing to it that the routine goes smoothly. In that way you are not only a favorite spot within its first-order home but also its reliable activity director and meal planner. That's the secret behind talking to a cat. Silly, the cat of an elderly couple who themselves disliked disruption in their daily routines, was from kittenhood enticed into the basement for the night with an evening meal and the whistled tune of "Danny Boy." The tune eventually sent Silly to the basement in anticipation of a meal whenever the couple wished.

Ordering the cat to the basement wouldn't have worked. Cats have no respect for authority. They are not cooperative and friendly pack animals. Give a cat a stern command and you are likely to be ignored or swatted. Put a choke collar on a cat to discipline it and you have a cat on its back with its claws and teeth raking your arm.

Yet house cats can learn all sorts of tricks if their environment is forthcoming and reliable. Ernie Dickinson, a friend and writer, has a stunning yellow cat named Georgie Pillson who, upon request, leaps through hoops, jumps from the floor into his arms, rolls over, and, upon hearing the jingle of car keys, runs to the door for a ride. Georgie walks in the woods with Ernie without a leash and shakes hands with strangers. He is now learning how to walk a tightrope and how to press his paw on an ink pad in preparation for signing this book when it is published. Ernie did not train Georgie by asserting his authority. He wooed him patiently, with bits of chicken liver.

"Cats are trained by rewarding them with food," Ernie said. "But once a trick is learned, praise and attention suffice. Georgie now rolls over for me without any reward except my applause and verbal praise. For that he will do it again and again."

However, Ernie admits that there are limitations to being a responsive environment. Georgie Pillson will not use the carpeted wooden cave Ernie made for him or a sleeping bag he gave to him, preferring three velvet chairs and the real beds. The house is, after all, his oddly piecemeal first-order environment, and if he chooses to ignore some aspect of it, that portion is not "there" to him.

Even professionals can't do much about the ultimate independence of the best-trained cats. A house cat who performed in a small traveling circus was so acrobatic that my son Craig bought me a ticket to his performance. He could hardly wait for my return to share with me his delight in this cat's astonishing skills.

"What's so great about a cat sleeping on the top of a stepladder?" I asked when I got home.

"Well, that's confusing," Craig said. "The cat leaped through hoops and turned flips in the air when I saw him last night."

A cat is like that. It is not a hail-fellow-well-met who will go along with any nutty activity its host suggests, as will a dog. Its attitude is that of a relative settling in, expecting concessions to be made on both sides.

WILL YOU BE MINE?

Like a relative who has come to stay, a cat soon makes itself at home by leaving its personal "belongings" around. Luckily, this is not still more empty glasses and old magazines to contend with but invisible and, to us, unsmellable pheromones, the cat's personal odor. Cats produce these pheromones in glands discovered by British scientist R. G. Prescott, who discerned their locations by noting those spots where cats touch and rub people, furniture, trees, and other "beloved

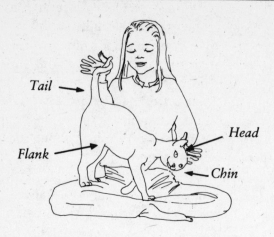

Tail

Head

Flank

Chin

The locations of pheromone glands

objects." The scent glands are in the head, along the lips, beneath the chin, and strung along the flank and tail.

Those odoriferous areas cats rub liberally on everything from people to posts. When they lace us with these friendly and intimate odors, they are labeling and stabilizing us in their environment. They perfume us with grace and often with contented purrs—as when Joan and Danny bumped heads. Because the touch seems loving, and often is, we tend to ignore the real point of the message. Pheromone rubbing is not so much an outgoing confession of love as it is the stamping of property with ownership labels.

But the more responsive you are to being marked as your cat's own object by stroking and rubbing in the right places, the more heavily you will be scented and the more beloved you will be. Those who avoid a cat's marking are flatly stating that they refuse to belong.

Cats can be quite miffed by such a rejection from their

environment and then all the more aggressively insist on having things their own way. Cats are wizards at sensing which people are trying to avoid them, and they rub pheromones on them ad nauseam until picked up and tossed away. Every time I walk into the apartment where Freud, a black cat with a white star on his chest, lives, I am rubbed to exasperation. If I stand and talk with his master, a psychiatrist friend of mine, Freud is around my ankles marking me with his chin, and if I sit down, he is on my lap rubbing his head and tail against me. I am forced to either throw him to the ground or spit at him in his own language, my teeth bared. Chastised, he waits under a chair until I am involved in conversation, then returns to harass me with pheromones. I never have achieved a decent relationship with that cat.

Cats also present their scent glands to other cats during courtship, to their young when mothering, and to siblings and mother when they are kittens. Scents thus serve as a bonding language in genuine social relationships, as well as a personal stamp on belongings. You can talk love and affection to your cat through these gland points even when the cat is not the initiator. Stroke the head, chin, flank, tail—you will be answered with a possessive purr.

SAY IT WITH A STARE

Beyond the cat's first-order home is the second-order one, less beloved but no less important to free-ranging cats. To a wild cat, the second-order home is the wider area that surrounds its central, best-loved, and most-frequented place. To the house cat it is beyond the house and garden, out in the surrounding yards, woods, and fields. You could call it the work area, for the second-order home is a network of trails that lead to grounds for hunting, courting, fighting, and other cat business. Cats who are protected from the dangers of such adventures by being kept indoors do not have second-order homes.

The outer limits of second-order trails for free-roaming cats can be an area half to one square kilometer for a female and twice that for an unaltered male. Just as cats have a sense of territory somewhat different from our concept of a specific area with an invisible fence drawn around it, so they do not share our attitude about protecting property, as do wolves and many other mammals. They don't mark boundaries and don't defend the area at all costs against others of the same species. As far as cats are concerned, all parts of their grounds (except for the den where babies are being raised) are there to be used by other cats on occasion, provided they occupy path or place one at a time and under the right conditions. The trouble is, the "conditions" are strictly personal. Trinket let one of the neighborhood cats sit on her favorite pillow in her first-order home—but only that cat and only when she wasn't occupying it.

All of the trails through second-order territory make sense. Their destinations are important to cat life. People who let their cats out of the house at night and think of them wandering the country on wild and nefarious expeditions are wrong. Cats have exact destinations in mind, take precise routes to these places, and return along them when the mission is completed. If the mission is mating, toms might not come home for a week or more. But cats are not lost. They know where they are and why they are there, and, unless hurt or "adopted" by others, they will return home. The cats that "come in out of the cold" and adopt you are usually cats that have been dropped along a street or road side and abandoned. They do not leave home and choose to live elsewhere unless they have been abused by other cats, dogs, or humans. Cats love their places and their pathways.

My backyard, on a wooded hillside in Chappaqua, New York, is laced with cat pathways originally laid down by Trinket and now used and sustained since her death by the neighborhood cats. The pathways are not visible like the trails of deer and the runways of mice. It is as if the cat had learned not to beat a path to the game and so betray its presence. The only way to find cat paths is to watch the cats walk along them. One trail in my yard threads beneath overhanging rhododendron, passes the edge of the flower garden, and arrives at the sandy area near the toolshed—a sunning spot. Another skirts the grape arbor and arrives in the small field beyond my woodpile, where mice abound. Only one crosses the open yard, and this would not be there were there a more secretive way to get to the bird feeder.

On their pathways cats avoid other cats at all costs. If by chance two arrive at a crossroads at the same time, a despicable situation, they prevent a confrontation by communicating with their eyes. No sound is uttered, nor are teeth bared. They stare, sending a message over as far as one hundred meters with their large eyes.

I saw the stare keep two toms from meeting while I was sitting with a friend on his roof patio in New York City. The two cats were walking across the rooftop on two different pathways destined to cross. One cat had a torn ear, the other a scarred cheek, attesting to their free-roaming life among scrapping city cats. They were on a collision course at a brisk pace. Anticipating a fight, I sat forward. Within two feet of the crossing both stopped, sat down, tucked their toes under their chests, and stared at each other.

After a long time, ten minutes at least, Torn Ear looked deliberately away—then back.

Several minutes later Scar Face looked away—then back.

The staring match

This went on for almost an hour, each staring and looking away, each feeling out the other and talking threat talk through the eyes. The tension was building. Torn Ear looked away for the umpteenth time, and Scar Face got to his feet. Hesitatingly at first, then swiftly, he ran down the path and dashed across the crossroads. He disappeared among the TV antennas surrounding a water tank. After sitting for another half hour, Torn Ear got up and followed the same path. Scar Face had won the battle of the eyes, but that was not the point. A confrontation had been averted.

STRONG MESSAGE

Even the discomfort of staring matches is often avoided by cats' form of scent marking. Cats spray urine to make their environment familiar and to leave messages for others.

Both sexes spray urine—the females spraying more rather than less than the males, but in smaller quantities. Since the structure of the female does not allow her to spray in jets, as does the male's anatomy, she simply emits droplets. Males spray by backing up to an object, lifting their tails high, and somehow turning their penises in such a way that the jet comes out parallel to the ground—and backwards! Tomcats, but not females, spray not only path and place within their second-order territory but also objects in their first-order home. Although full of subtlety and pleasantly odoriferous to the cat, cat urine simply stinks to us. The smell of urine from unaltered pets is particularly strong and hard to eradicate. Altered pets, which no longer produce the hormones that advertise their sexuality, have milder urine, and the males don't spray the house.

As for the meaning of spraying—a bit of spray exuded on strange territory fills the air with the reassuring scent of self and gives cats confidence to proceed. Their own spray evidently also gives cats great pleasure. Trinket would spray and then return sometime later to sniff and rub her head in the odor as if enjoying herself in the way a pretty woman admires her reflection in a mirror. At the same time, the odors are messages to other cats; they say that the marker is nearby or has passed that way. Apparently the intensity of the odor tells the reader how recently the marker passed by, and it can help the reader judge whether or not it is prudent to continue along that path or sit and wait for the scent marker to finish its business and leave the vicinity. Cats sitting for hours under a bush are not necessarily hunting. Very often they are sniffing fading pheromones and waiting for the air to clear, so to speak. The scent is certainly not a keep-off-the-property odor, as is the dog's or wolf's, for I have seen both males and females sniff a post that Trinket marked and sit down quite contentedly nearby, even when she was not in heat.

We do know that urine messages bring mates together, however. A female's spray is droplets full of news of her sexual readiness. She tells the males that estrus is beginning and gives them progress reports; they answer in kind. In addition, she states who she is, how old she is, and her mood. Cat urine varies in strength according to the emotion of the cat. An angry cat and a neglected cat emit strong urine whose odor is a concentrated essence of their mood.

Certain odors, usually sexual, when inhaled evoke a strange and sort of disgusted-looking grimace and noise called *flehmen,* a German word with no English counterpart. The cat sniffs, sometimes touches the scent substance with its tongue as well, then raises its head, pulls back its lips, wrinkles its nose, inhales deeply, and holds its breath. The strange sniff is a thorough examination of the material by both the taste buds and the nose; it is the quintessential sniff.

We probably miss most such expressions, since a cat is more likely to come upon an intensely interesting odor in its outdoor wanderings than in its first-order home, but occasionally a cat will *flehmen* if you have been with another cat. How your cat reacts to such news depends on whose odor you have brought home. Danny never failed to suck in, pull back his lips, wrinkle his nose, and gag when Joan brought home the odor of Jerry, an enemy. Danny was not so much angry at Joan for visiting his enemy as at the cat who was there in pheromones. Smell is reality to a cat.

House cats and many of their small wild cousins generally bury their feces. When they don't, leaving them instead out in the open, they are intended as communication. Apparently feces on display are simple statements, for while cats investigate them with some curiosity, they neither run away from nor actively seek out the sender. Perhaps they are "ain't-

I-somethin' " posters. Morris Hornocker, wildlife professor of the University of Idaho, reports that the Canada lynx and the puma not only deposit feces in the open for others of their kind to read but kick up snow and earth to set them upon—the better to display them. In Big Cypress Swamp, Florida, I found a bobcat's feces conspicuously deposited on a mound of once-beautiful royal ferns that the animal had kicked and trampled into a pile. I think I responded to the message just as another bobcat might have done. Wow! Look at that, thought I.

Feces left out for people to see can, as some of us know, be a blue-funk message. Danny left such a statement on Joan's favorite chair after she punished him for getting up on the table and eating the fish fillet. Trinket deposited the same remark on my daughter's bed when she brought home a stray cat.

If fecal messages can be resentful, scratch messages can be downright vindictive. To keep their front claws honed, cats scratch furniture and trees to remove the outer cover of their weapons, peeling them down to sharpness much as we sharpen pencils with a knife. They bite off the claw covers of their rear paws. Sharpening the claws, then, is a preparation for killing, and as such it becomes a declaration of war. Danny often sharpened his claws after Joan scolded him. He would run to the chair upholstered in needlepoint, reach as high as he could, twitch his tail, unsheathe his claws, and dig in. The sounds of threads breaking as he dragged the length of the chair arm were terrible to hear. At other times he claw sharpened to show Joan how strong and wonderful he was. He would wait until she was watching him, then his back would ripple and his eyes would soften; the meriow he gave as he dug in was the sound of the courting tom. She had answers for both scratched communications—a maga-

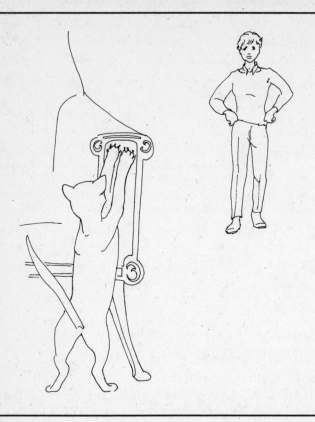

zine rattled and tossed in his direction.

Claw sharpening is carefully observed by other cats. The neighbor's black cat would sit under a bush and stare at Trinket when she tore grooves into the apple tree. When she was done, he would get up and walk away, with apparent lack of interest, only to mosey back later to read her grooves. No doubt the height of grooves gives an indication of the maker's size, and the depth a measure of its strength.

Occasionally the cat's hind feet get into a scratched communication in what is known as *paw wiping*. The cat vig-

orously scratches the ground with the hind paws. It is an act of extreme hostility because the back feet are used primarily for vaulting the animal forward into battle or tearing open the belly of an opponent. When they are used, it is serious talk—of a kind that some people can get into with some cats. Joe, a hired man on our Pennsylvania farm, kept the tomcat out of the kitchen by wiping his feet and standing broadside to him, as cats stand to others when paw wiping. The tom would take stock of the movement and, ears pressed to his head, slink off along the wall of the house, headed for the barn.

TALK TO ME OF LOVE

It is a seeming paradox that although cats despise each other and avoid contact whenever possible, they truly need our attention. Cats must get affection from the person or persons they live with, or they become depressed and will not groom themselves. A cat that is simply given food may live, but it is usually dirty and seedy looking.

The paradox dissolves on closer inspection. No matter how solitary the fashion in which an animal must earn its living as a hunter, it must be social enough to mate and to raise a family.

In the wild, female cats accompany their kittens during their first five months of life in order to adequately train them to hunt alone. Since they give birth every year, they are by themselves only a little more than half the time. There is also evidence that female relatives—mothers, daughters, and sisters—share a territory more closely than males. Witch, a "house" cat who scorned a roof over her head, produced annual litters simultaneously with her grown daughter. While her daughter nursed both her own and her mother's kittens, Witch hunted for the whole extended family. What's more, Paul Leyhausen noted that his females tended to mate with favorite males. Other observers, too, have thought that free-roaming females prefer to mate again and again with the same male if they are allowed the choice. Trinket's many litters looked a lot like Belknap, a gray-and-white tom in the neighborhood, and we assumed she was faithful to him. Although males do not help raise the young, some do pay calls on their family. Belknap turned up at the door with a chipmunk one day right after his kittens were born. Cats do love.

In fact, because we have to confine or alter males and females to control their prodigious reproductive rate, we may cut off natural social interludes in cats' otherwise solitary lives, leaving them lonely as well as loners.

Occasionally cats get together outdoors in an odd catlike manner that is perhaps an awkward attempt to socialize. They gather in considerable numbers, sitting well spaced with their feet tucked under them, smiling in some sort of cat communion. This is about as much of a concession as cats give to cat social events, and after a few hours they become bored, get up, and walk away. Such a gathering took place in a field near the station platform in White Plains, New York, at least once a week during a spring when I commuted early enough to see it. At about an hour after sunrise, I could see cats coming from all directions—out of the parking lot, down the street, meandering from the row houses, and strolling up from the streambed along the tracks. They were dignified, walked slowly, and used their eyes to settle spatial quarrels. Now and then one would spit to hold its place. They were always gone when I came back at the end of the day.

In your house you fill social needs by simply being there. Most times social contact is casual, but it can be passionate, as when Danny demanded the attention of Joan after her two-day absence

It is that passionate demand that is so startling in so aloof a creature. Geneticists suggest an explanation. The genetic change that relaxed the adult cat's wariness of humans affected, they believe, maturity in general. The young of most mammals are curiously unafraid and only playfully aggressive. That mildness is eventually overwhelmed by the more cautious and defensive behaviors acquired in adulthood. Domestic cats, it seems, do not develop fear and fury toward people. Without that the domestic cat reveals to us a kitten's affection for its mother, a mother's devotion to her young, and a lover's passion for its mate.

Most of a house cat's vocabulary of affection is derived from kitten expressions. By watching mother and young, the entire vocabulary can be seen and interpreted as she and her kittens, and they among themselves, interact, using the mews, poses, and actions that the grown cat later lavishes on its persons.

BACK TO THE CRADLE

The pregnant house cat is true to her wild heritage. She picks a den in her first-order home in which to give birth to her young. The den may be a closet, basket, box, or some nook among the ducts and rafters in the basement. Most females, having established a nest, tend to return to it year after year. Trinket's birthing den was the clothes closet in Twig's room. She demanded shirts, socks, and blue jeans for nesting material by scratching the floor of the closet and meowing loudly.

Some cats give birth so privately that the event is only discovered by happening upon the kittens. Others want at-

Announcing the hour of birth

tendance. Trinket announced the hour of birth to us by mewing, running toward the nest, coming back if we did not follow, and running forward again. She could hold back the birth for several hours while she gathered her human friends. Many of my friends report that they, too, are called to their house cat's birthing. As far as is known, no wild or feral cats behave that way. They give birth alone and in silence. Perhaps it is the kitten in domestic cats that wants attention from the mother in us at this time.

Immediately after a kitten is born, and sometimes while the hind end is still in the birth channel, the mother licks open its nostrils and cleans the mucus and blood from its fur.

Some people object to a cat's licking them, because of the roughness of the tongue. But licking speaks of the intimate relationship that originated between mother and kitten, and it is bestowed upon people who fill that special role of family in a cat's life. It is more than affection; it is bonding and should be endured with that in mind.

Kittens are born appealingly furry, but the eyes are closed as well as the ears, so communication must be largely by touch. We ourselves find them so adorable that we can hardly resist fondling and holding them, but they also speak warmly to one another. Before birth, the skin around the mother's mammary glands has lost its fur and become highly vascularized so that the nipple area is softly nude and very warm. When the mother enters the nest, her kittens crowd to her belly and, having located by touch and scent their preferred nipple (which they keep for the duration of nursing), knead at it with their forepaws to stimulate the let-down of milk. Leyhausen calls this the *milk tread*.

The kneading of your adult cat's paws on your lap or arm goes back to the relationship between mother and young and is a request for comfort.

Although usually a warm and friendly gesture, the milk tread can also be hurtful and demanding. Trinket on occasion at night while I slept would leap onto my stomach and begin to softly knead, demanding something—usually to go out. If I ignored her, the pressure became harder and harder, and the purr would shift into a purr-snarl. If I still did not get up, the kneading became so strong that it actually hurt, and I would be forced out of bed to open the window and let her onto her pathway that led across the roof and down the lilac bush.

For the first few days of life, kittens huddle together, one head upon the neck of another, in a compact circle. If the mother runs off and a kitten is still attached to her nipple, it may drop quite far from the nest with its circular snuggle of kittens. It finds its way back by an inherited, but seemingly intelligent, behavior. It mews pitifully, a high-pitched tone incessantly repeated. If this fails to bring the mother, the kitten begins a miraculous search for home. It crawls with shaky movements, not on a straight line, which might not be the right direction, but in a spiral. By spiraling in an ever-widening circle, it gets home eventually. A cat will also spiral your lap or a soft pillow as if looking for the center of the snuggle target.

For her part, a mother cat draws her kittens into a group with her paws. This all-in-the-family gesture is also practiced on humans. When a cat is picked up and hugged by a member of the household, it will pull in its claws, cup the paw, and extend the whole foot up and around the shoulder as if drawing the person into the circle as it was drawn into the kitten group by its mother. William, although a male, uses the same gesture to bring Sara's arm into the circle of the nest he occupies in her lap.

Less delightful is the bumping way of begging that kittens develop as they are weaned. Trinket's kittens begged for milk by running alongside her at full speed, bumping against her flanks as they traveled and knocking her off her course. Adult cats are whizzes at using this begging behavior on people, dashing along beside and bumping against us until we grant their request, trip over them, or toss them out the door.

MEOWS AND PURRS

To the uninitiated, the cat's meow is a single all-purpose word that means everything from the food that cats "ask for by name" to a request for sexual attention. Actually, there are numerous meows that differ in pitch, rhythm, loudness, tone, and "pronunciation," and each has a different meaning or is spoken only under certain circumstances.

A mother cat, for instance, greets her litter with a chirruping sound whenever she returns to the nest. She does this from their earliest hours, when it is doubtful they can hear her through their still-sealed ears. That chirruped meow, rendered *mierrrow* with the *r*'s, burbled, is a great compliment when directed to a human, for it is an intensely affectionate and personal greeting. Uttered with a greater passion—and often so incessantly as to drive one to distraction—it is meant as a come-on. The cat wishes to mate. In other words, some degree of intimacy is always implied by the chirruped *mierrrow*.

A kitten's first sound is *mew*. It is weak, high-pitched, and brief during the first days, a complaint at being separated from the huddle and a plea for help. This mew remains as the polite form of request but also develops into the more demanding—or even commanding—meow. In its superpolite form, mew is actually soundless, a mere miming with no participation of the vocal cords. The mouth opens, the head goes back, all the gestures of mewing are there, but no sound comes out. Several cat owners interpret the silent plea as a smug way of demanding food at the table without being obnoxious; others find it to be part of the telepathy between a cat and its special person.

Trinket mimed soundlessly with mouth open to announce her presence among her kittens when she and they were at peace—which says something for the telepathy interpretation.

The paws also send messages through the floor or ground, for the cat does not always walk quietly as the fog on those "little cat feet." Trinket called her kittens by striking the floor when she felt a meow was too loud and dangerous for the occasion. She also used the floorboard telegraph when the house was noisy with talking people and her meow could not carry above the din. Apparently the vibrations could carry, and she would thump up the steps, sending signals through the wood to her kittens in the closet. The kittens would feel the message, awake, and run to meet her.

I eventually learned to call the kittens with a tap on the floor, but never Trinket. Apparently the adult cat outgrows its response to this command, although it still gives it. William, whose only experience of kittenhood was his own, thumps out a heavy message on his way downstairs to call his family to dinner. That is, they are to assemble to give *him* dinner. At twenty pounds the message is loud, yet the huge cat can pussyfoot the stairs when he wants to.

When vocalized, the meow comes off the forward part of the tongue—the same place where we shape our imitation meows. It is used all through life when asking for care, such as a bowl of food, or to be picked up and caressed, or for other instructional messages. The basic request is made while the cat looks at you; it is a repeated series of smooth whines that actually sound like begging.

But the expression varies considerably with the intensity of the cat's felt need. The loud, clipped meow is a demand: "Let me out of this house" or "There is no water in my bowl."

Cat lovers who really listen to their cats can distinguish a more extreme form of demand meow that might add to the request to be let out—the further distress note "I have to pee right now." Patricia Moyes, author of *How to Talk to Your Cat,* describes such a demand meow as "high-pitched, sustained, incessantly repeated and absolutely infuriating." Of course, that's why it works.

Moyes further distinguishes the complaint—"basically the high-pitched demand, but laced with a plaintive, falling cadence"; the protest—"the equivalent of a child's whining—a plaintive, high-to-low cadence, uttered without too much conviction and much lower in pitch than the complaint"; and indignation—"the chief characteristic [of which] is self-righteousness. It is a single high note uttered in short, sharp syllables and indicates that the cat has a legitimate grouse that he feels would stand up in a court of law."

Trinket had at least five different meows when she talked to her kittens. The two most understandable were loud—one that meant, "Follow me," and a sharp nasal one that meant, "Stop it." If I imitated her "Stop-it" command when she got up on the table, she would jump right down.

She used a high-pitched, open-mouthed meow to call the kittens to solid food, a sharp growl-mierow to send them to cover. I learned to imitate the growl-mierow, hoping to keep Trinket's kittens off the road, but I never had to use it. She had already communicated the hazards of roads and cars. They hid at the sound of a motor.

The whole series of meows, from timid request to arrogant command, is easier to understand than to describe. Most cat owners can tell by context what a cat wants and how badly, for it won't urgently request to be let out while

MEOW CHART

Kittens have only one word, but its intensity is a clue to the urgency of their need.

mew (high-pitched and thin)	A polite plea for help
MEW! (loud and frantic)	An urgent plea for help, as when the kitten is lost

Adult cats elaborate on the basic mew and make their meaning clearer by poses, gestures, and context.

mew	A plea for care and/or attention
mew (soundless)	The very civilized, polite form of the plea
meow	The somewhat more demanding, begging form of the plea
MEOW!	A command to give care and/or attention
mee-o-ow (with a falling cadence)	A protest equivalent to a child's whine when he has not gotten what he wanted
MEE-o-ow (whined, but shrill)	A stronger protest

sitting next to the can opener, nor will it mew politely for food at the door. Still, for the most interested, a tape recorder is a good way to catch, play back, and memorize subtle differences. Some who have also recorded their cat's greeting to them have discerned that it can be the equivalent of a name. Just as you have a personal call for your cat—"William" or "Here, kitty"—your cat has a personal call for you. Taping it will help you to recognize it, for it is always the same unique meow.

When kittens' eyes and ears open at about five to ten

MYUP! (short, sharp, single note)	Righteous indignation
MEOW! MEOW! *MEOW! MEOW!*	A panicky call for help, as when the cat is being molested
mier-r-r-ow (chirruped with a lilting cadence)	The "hello" greeting, implies intimacy when uttered with passion

Tom cats have a vocabulary of their own.

RR-YOWWWW- *EEOW-RR-YOW-* *OW*	Night song when on the sexual prowl, known as the caterwaul
merrrow	Call to a young male to come out and fight
meriow	Courting call to female

Mother cats have special calls used only with their kittens.

MEE OW	Call to come for food
meOW	Call to follow
ME R-R-R-ROW	Call to run to cover
mer ROW!	"No!" or "Stop it!"
mreeeeep (burbled)	The "Hello" greeting to kittens and the kittens' disarming greeting to adult cats

days old, they begin to be able to cry in panic. Moyes describes
the adult's panic cry as "a frantic squawk . . . [that is] blood-
chilling and [that] must be taken seriously." The cat is in
trouble—the neighborhood kids have tied a tin can to its tail.
Kittens panic under less dire threats. A kitten calls frantically
if it is lost, stuck behind the sofa, or being attacked or trampled by siblings. It is a long-distance cry. Trinket could hear
it from upstairs when we brought a kitten downstairs to play
with and admire—a circumstance she was likely to interpret
as a kitten either lost or under attack. She would come to its

"rescue" on the run, calling the growl-mierow "Run-to-cover"
command, which, in this context, we took also to mean,
"Give me back my baby."

The purr distinguishes cats of every kind from all other
animals. It is unique in nature. Charles Darwin wrote that of
all the feline sounds, "the purr of satisfaction, which is made
both during inspiration and expiration, is one of the most
curious." Lonely people feel wanted and good again when
their cat purrs in their laps; it is a sound that needs no translation. The little girl across the street heard Trinket purr for
the first time and told me my cat was smiling out loud. And
so she was. Of the approximately sixteen different sounds the
cat makes to express emotions and desires, the purr is the
only one that conveys luscious contentment.

What is particularly wonderful about the purr is that it
is given only in the presence of another animal. A lone cat
sitting in the window does not purr, no matter how content.
Cat purrs are communications, and cats are too sane to talk
to themselves.

Purring is first heard when the kitten is about two days
old and nursing. From that first contentment purr, the sound
develops a more varied range of expression and meaning. A
single purr announces that a pleasurable contact has been
made—you have touched the cat's head or back for an instant—whereas a rhythmical purr repeated like an ABA song
form (A: *rrrr*, B: [cranked a bit higher] *rrrrr*, A: *rrrr*) declares
that the cat is being held and generously petted. When the
cat is wonderfully content, it can purr loud enough to be
heard across a room. But the classic ABA purr is only one of
several murmur sounds that are made in the throat and that,
in varying intensities, signify either lessening contentment or
rising excitement. When an ordinary purr trips over into a
purr-snarl, it says, "Enough of this sweetness. I'm annoyed."

Heightened excitement is expressed by the abrupt loud purr given by a female when she is ready to be inseminated. That word is not spoken to humans.

BUZZ OFF, FELIX

A mark of our distinction among cats is that they so often direct to us their positive statements and so seldom their negative ones. We expect dogs to resent our entry into their territory, but when was the last time a cat growled at you?

Cats are not so tolerant of one another.

It is not that cats cannot live together in a human household. They do, even purring in concert and grooming each other, but such cats are usually litter mates, or one of the pair was introduced as a kitten. Only on rare occasions do adults adjust to each other peaceably in the same household. Any cat given its druthers prefers to live alone with you.

To understand what would happen to your cat if it had to depend on another cat for sociability, you need only to observe an encounter between two strange cats.

Riley is large and yellow, and he is battered—a sign to other cats that he has survived many battles and has the nicks and scars to prove it. He met the staid, black Parson when two friends of mine together rented a mountain cabin for the summer.

On their arrival the carrying cases were opened at the same time. The cats ran out and faced each other across the room. As if by agreement they both turned away and inspected the new environment to establish their first-order home. But the question of who was boss soon overshadowed even that important duty. After a brief look at the surroundings they faced the real problem: each other.

First they sniffed nose to nose without touching—the

initial part of the cat greeting that every cat owner is familiar with. It is said to you when the cat jumps in your lap and lifts its head toward your nose, sometimes sweetly touching for a moment. If it is feeling particularly friendly, it will turn its rear end toward you for an anal sniff. This is an honor that most people shun.

Red Riley and black Parson were not going to honor each other with anal presentations. They stood apart, sniffing noses faster and faster. Angrily they closed their whiskers tightly against their faces. Both lowered their hindquarters a little bit and equally. Moments passed; they tilted their heads at an angle. They held their ears erect and faced each other, feet planted firmly. They stared the threat stare—pupils dilated, eyes wide, the lips lifted slightly. Each was trying to psych out the other, like wrestlers in the opening moments of a match.

Parson wore down first. He lowered his haunches ever so slightly. Had these two been wise cats, that would have ended the battle for dominance. Those lowered haunches foretold the outcome, for the gesture is made by the loser. I had seen Trinket use this code on me when I reprimanded her for being on the table. She was saying. "You win."

Parson's admission, however, did not end the conversation. Riley was aching for battle, and Parson responded. They moved in closer until each could sniff the nape of the other's neck, the prey's death spot that every cat knows so well. They felt each other's nape with their whiskers, as if through these—their stethoscopes—they could measure the impulses of nerves running along the spinal cord.

The sniffing of the napes moved to the flanks. Riley was in charge. He had not missed the lowering of Parson's rear end, and he was confident. He showed his confidence by lifting his tail and granting Parson an anal sniff.

The odor and the act of his self-assurance put Parson on the defensive. He flattened his ears, twisted them back and down, and crouched. Forced to look up at Riley, he was at a disadvantage and, now aroused to fear, acted to protect himself. He growled. Low-pitched at the outset, Parson's growl, like all cat growls, was a curious sustained noise coming from the back of the throat that rolled out louder and louder—a sound that falls somewhere between a dog's growl and a very deep meow.

Then Parson struck Riley on the nose. It seemed that he was the aggressor, so furiously did he strike, but that was not so. The paw strike is a defensive action, and it gave the black cat time to turn and run far enough away to feel somewhat more secure. He pivoted and faced his still-serene rival.

Riley walked to the spot where Parson had been sitting and sniffed. "I'm in charge," he was reiterating, as he lingered long over the odor, before slowly approaching Parson. Head high, tail twitching, Riley went through the greeting ceremony again, sniffing nose, flank, and anal area. This was an insult. The greeting was being used to rub in his superiority.

Parson felt the psychological bruise. He answered with the spit, that sharp hissing sound that we use ourselves when angry and frustrated. We also use the same facial expression as the spitting cat—lips curled up to expose the teeth, nose wrinkled, eyes slanted downward.

Having spit out his wrath, Parson turned and slunk off, and as he did so, spots on the backs of his ears, which some cats have, gleamed like eyes. They are called *threat spots* and can disconcert a rival. Riley saw them and hesitated just long enough for Parson to jump to the top of the couch.

His height reversed their roles; Parson now was, literally, in a position of dominance. He eyeballed Riley. Riley sat down and looked away.

When at last Parson forgot the feud and jumped down from the couch for dinner, Riley ran out from behind a door where he was waiting and watching, biffed the black cat across the face with a paw, and rolled beneath him.

He had gained the offensive position in a cat fight. Slashing his unsheathed claws, he raked the belly of wailing Parson and slashed his elbow with his teeth. When fighting each other, cats are programmed to cut the elbow with their teeth, not grab the death site at the nape of the neck. They will injure but not kill each other, except in rare instances of error. Bloodcurdling screams issued from both cats, and then they broke apart.

After a pause Riley attacked again. There was no breaking them up without my friends' getting slashed and bitten. Tufts of fur flew through the air, claws ripped in movements too swift to see. When they broke apart this time, Riley was clearly and permanently the dominant cat. Parson thereafter put his ears back and down in his presence.

They never fought again, but Riley would not let the subdued Parson forget who had won. If Parson walked within twenty feet of him, Riley gave him the threat stare and growled or spit. Parson would lower his head, neck, and ears and slink off. They never got along, but they had arrived at a working arrangement. Parson had to stay away.

Apparently cats never think of even bossy owners as rivals or enemies, for they reserve their growls, hisses, and spits for the vet who must do a painful examination or for a person who abuses them. Female cats do, however, speak to their owners quite passionately of sexual love.

THE SEXY COME-ON

An unaltered female confined to the house without a partner flirts with her human friends, both male and female, as she comes into heat. She rubs her head on the floor in their direction and lies broadside to say, "I choose you as my love."

As the estrous period advances, the days pass in many such graceful mating overtures until she is ready to be inseminated. Then she announces her condition by lying on her belly, forelegs outstretched from the elbows, her neck extended above them. Her eyes narrow to a seductive slit. Her ears are folded daintily back. Her rump is raised, her knees are practically on the ground, her heels are up as she lifts her rear on tiptoes, ups her tail, and holds it to the side. Trinket would talk to my daughter in the mating language even when she wasn't in estrus by directing one or all of these movements toward her. It was a language we learned to read and which Twig found very flattering. She would answer Trinket's overtures with soft words and strong kneading down the back like the caresses of the tom.

You can elicit similarly sensual behavior in most cats with catnip, the one means by which humans can communicate with their pet through scent. Catnip, a weed to some and a valued herb or ornamental to others, contains a volatile

oil that, it is suspected, in some way resembles cat sex pheromones. The Japanese plant *matatabi*, the silvervine, and one of the garden heliotropes of Europe also contain volatiles that have an erotic effect on cats. Although some cats are not susceptible to these odors, most cats, of both sexes and regardless of whether or not they have been altered, go into an exotic performance, rolling and slithering as if courting. They claw, clutch, rub, and lick a toy stuffed with catnip.

John Henry, an Abyssinian kitten, went into similar conniptions over a perfumed guest. The perfume was Tabu.

Trinket was a beautiful dancer when she was given her catnip-filled mouse. She would rub her neck on the floor, slide along on her shoulder, then roll to her side with a thump, jump up, bat the toy, pounce, and go through the sensual

"Be my love."

routine again—very much like the routine she performed when she was in heat. Her reaction to the catnip, however, did not bring on her period of estrus, as some people might believe. When I took it away, she was no closer to mating than before the plant fatale was presented.

Alluring poses and gestures are only part of the mating vocabulary. We seldom get to see the rest of it, for cats usually mate at night. With persistence, however, I was able to take notes on one of Trinket's beautiful conversations with her mate, Belknap.

Toms have sexual periodicity, although not as definite or obvious as the females, so they are not always ready to mate. When this particular courtship began, Belknap, attracted by Trinket's estrous perfume, had arrived at our porch, but he was not very interested. Trinket took the initiative. She rubbed her neck on the floor, then she rubbed her shoulder, rolled onto her side with a thump, and faced her lover sideways. She had to repeat this seductive performance over and over for several days before Belknap began to show interest by spraying.

He brought Trinket a present, a mouse that she coyly hugged to her belly while lying on her back. She kicked the mouse with all four feet and batted at it with her forepaws. While she played, Belknap pounced on her. She was not ready. She swatted him and leaped away. They locked paws, rolled, got up, and chased each other up and down the front steps and around the bushes. They scrambled up tree trunks a ways and dropped back to earth. Now I understood that some of Trinket's games of chase with us were not just play but also the flirtation of courtship.

After days of chase and no action, Belknap became bored. He stalked off the porch to the garden. Trinket ran up to him and rubbed her head against his. That aroused his interest

again. He attempted to mount her. She fended him off with
a blow, screaming and shrieking as though he had attacked
her. Belknap moved away, but not far. He sat under a small
maple, keeping an eye on her. He mewed from time to time
and, as males do during courtship to release tension, rattled
his teeth together. He had not been home for six days. I
brought them both inside to be fed. They were not interested.

Just before sunset Trinket gave the sharp purr-snarl that
said she was ready. She looked demurely over her shoulder
at Belknap. He stepped over her, placing his feet carefully
alongside her body and gently taking hold of the nape of her
neck with his teeth. Unlike the solid grip used in killing prey,
he seemed to hold skin only. Despite the steadying grip, Trinket
was not centered right beneath him. He stepped on her back
and gave her the milk tread on the spine—the one Twig used.
She righted herself squarely under him, and he, putting both
hind feet on the ground, growled as he thrust. After a few
thrusts he abruptly penetrated. She shrieked. The male penis
is covered with horny spines, but it is not clear whether the
female shrieks in pain or in ecstasy. At any rate, copulation
is brief, and Belknap withdrew after only seconds.

His genetic code passed on, Belknap jumped off backwards and dashed away. Trinket turned and swatted at him,
but he ignored her and sat quietly by. After a rest he took
the initiative and began the long courtship again.

They copulated at least three times in the two days that
I observed, but I could not be in attendance all the time; it
was probably much more.

Whenever Belknap's interest flagged, Trinket, in spite of
her apparent protest and pain, would motivate him anew by
presenting her rear end, kneading the ground, looking at him
over her shoulder, and even erecting hairs around the vulva
to attract his attention and accentuate the target.

Finally, seven days after the courtship had begun and at the end of Trinket's forty-eight-hour ovulation period, the mating was completed and Belknap disappeared.

Based on the similarity of all Trinket's litters to Belknap, we believe that she was faithful to that single mate. But no one can say just how loyal or disloyal cats are, for they usually seek each other out in the darkness and cannot be observed. It is also known that if one male becomes exhausted during the breeding period or is dragged home and locked up, other toms will take over his job. It is this, more than anything else, that gives the female a reputation among people of being morally loose and the male the reputation of tomcatting.

Tomcats are, however, noisy in their ardor and fiercely competitive with one another. Just after sundown, when the mating cat's day begins, toms court fights as well as females. A coaxing *merrrow* given by boss toms lures young males out to fight.

Soon the caterwauling begins—that banshee call in the night that draws showers of curses and missiles from people whose sleep is disturbed. Even one tom caterwauling is enough to wake the dead. A group of rivals caterwauling is indescribable. Scientists think the call is to a female and yet concede that it does not seem to have an immediate effect upon her. Trinket never turned her head when the tomcats caterwauled, but hours later, before dawn, she would give the demand meow to say she wanted to go out.

THE COMING-OUT PARTY

Even a rather aloof female house cat becomes unusually affectionate during pregnancy, as though preparing herself for the social demands of rearing kittens. Yet family life, that most sociable of times in a female's life, is brief with house cats.

The kittens, after a rollicking, tumbling kittenhood, are weaned with biffs and hisses and left to seek their solitary fortunes around three months of age.

There was a sharp contrast between Trinket's fiercely protective behavior when we brought a kitten downstairs to admire before she felt it was ready to leave the nest, and her equally fierce rejection of her kittens at weaning.

Trinket's rescue of her kittens began with a leap onto our laps. She would then weave her head back and forth as she honed in with eyes, nose, and ears on her young. With care she would grasp it by the nape of the neck, taking several test holds as if making certain she did not have the fatal grip of the cat on its prey. That the cat picks up its kittens with the same grip with which it makes a kill is worrisome until you realize that there is an automatic protection device. Nerves to the jaw pass on the "kitten" message, and the jaws lock apart. The murderous canine teeth are unable even to penetrate the skin.

After obtaining the right hold, Trinket would swing to the floor and, as she rushed up the stairs, beat out the foot tattoo to the other kittens: "I am coming."

Cats move their kittens frequently, not only for the purpose of good sanitation but also for the purpose of entering them into a broader environment for learning. The dark nest in the closet was good enough for wobbly offspring with thin mews and almost inaudible purrs, but when the kittens could meow for attention and had begun to play, Trinket carried them into the upstairs hallway and deposited them in the middle of the rug. Here they interacted with us, but only occasionally, because most of our family action was downstairs. The meetings were kindergarten lessons about people.

Gradually, as they became confident, she moved the kittens closer and closer to the main activity of the house.

When the kittens were something over a month old, she

carried them into the center of our life and deposited them in the middle of the living room floor. Here they learned the meaning of their mother's "No," the sharp *merROW*. It is clearly a no and possibly the reason that the domestic cat responds to our similar sound. Not only do theirs and ours both occur as sharp, short noises, but our faces have the same expressions when the admonishment is given. The forehead wrinkles, the mouth opens, and the eyebrows draw together. Trinket said no to such mischief as approaching the dog too closely, straying too far from the group, or disappearing altogether behind the couch.

The center of the living room floor was also the spot for the cat debut, a bittersweet ceremony held during the weaning period when the family is being prepared to break up and become loners. Swiss ethologist Rudolf Schenkel observed the debut among free-ranging lions in Africa. When the lion cubs are between three and four months old, the mother leads them from their nest in a dense thicket and across the savanna to meet the pride. As they cross the grassland, the adult members of the pride—sisters to the mother, young males, the father of the cubs—arise and wait quietly. The mother leads the cubs into the center of the gathering. The adults examine them with their eyes, ears, and noses, and occasionally with a gentle paw. Through all their senses they learn about the newest members of the pride—their sex, strength, and personalities. When satisfied they go back to what they were doing, which, with lions, is usually sleeping. Whereas before the debut the adult members of the pride usually have been bickering among themselves, all fighting ceases once they meet the cubs. It is much like the silence that ensues when a child enters a family argument.

The debut of the domestic cat is very similar. Only the pride is different; it is people.

On the day of the event Trinket would let us know it

was about to begin by wandering among us meowing softly, but demandingly. When she had gotten our attention, she would run upstairs, call, "Follow me," to her kittens, and parade them down the steps and into the center of the living room rug. There she would crouch with her feet under her. The kittens would look up at us and give us the silent meow. The first three or four times, we were not aware of what was going on, but because the kittens were so cute, we instinctively did the right thing. We picked them up and admired them. When I finally discovered Schenkel's research, many generations of kittens were off on their own with our blessings, even though we had not known we had given them.

With our new knowledge the last several litters were given grand debuts. All three children and I held the kittens,

The debut

sniffed their noses, and rubbed their heads. We stroked them on the tail, flank, and behind the ears to say in their own language that we were pleased with them. We also voiced our approval with high-pitched baby talk—sounds very close to cat sounds. My son Craig went one better. He lay on the rug sideways to them with his arm extended like a courting cat. There was no evidence that they were moved by this talk.

When we were done, or when Trinket thought we were, she led the kittens upstairs. Whereas before the debut she had conducted weaning mostly by noncooperation, nursing less frequently and more briefly than the kittens would have liked, she now said no to the first one that tried to nurse. Her irritation increased with each effort. *MYUP!*, she would complain when sick of saying the no *merROW*. If a kitten still persisted, she put an end to all demands with a spit or a growl. After the debut she paid less and less attention to them, and they wandered the house at will, filling the rooms with the wonderful sounds and sights of kittens.

Trinket's job was not yet over, however. All wild cats and many house cats train their kittens to hunt before bidding them a final good-bye. Trinket began by bringing a dead mouse to the nest when the kittens were about six weeks old, just before their weaning was begun. She would pick it up and drop it several times, growl over it, and then eat it, making no attempt to share with the kittens. A week later the kittens would sniff the mouse, drag it around, suck it, and also growl over it. At this point Trinket would bring a live mouse to the nest. She would now intersperse growls with soft coaxing purrs that stimulated the kittens to come forward and sniff. If she released the mouse, she would quickly recapture it as if to show them what to do. But, curiously, kittens do not take a mouse, alive or dead, by the nape of the neck at first. Like puppies that fight to establish their rank in the litter, kittens brawl during this period. Leyhausen thinks the killing bite does not develop until the kittens have established their pecking order and, with the fighting over, are no longer in danger of killing each other.

By three months, when the kittens were able to kill a mouse by themselves, Trinket was ready to let them go on their own into the world. In the wild, kittens would stay with their mother for months longer, following her along her hunting paths and honing by experience their innate hunting behaviors. That kittens are geared for months of practice is evident when you bring a kitten home, for much of kittenish behavior is actually hunting rehearsals.

PLAYING CAT AND MOUSE

The house cat is an incredibly gifted hunter. It rarely misses, for its technique is not chase and overcome like the canids, but lie in wait, stalk, and then pounce only when there is no other outcome for the prey but death. Much of a kitten's play with us is a game of hunt in which we act both as the mother providing practice prey and as the prey itself.

Many cats do not outgrow these games. All the games Trinket played with vigor and exuberance as a kitten were still exciting to her as an old cat. That she continued to respond with kittenish enthusiasm convinced me that the geneticists are correct; the house cat is forever retarded in youth.

Cats are not the devastating bird killers they are reputed to be, simply because birds are too hard to catch. Cats get discouraged when they fly off, and soon give up. A Polish scientist analyzed the stomach contents of 500 feral cats killled by hunters. His findings exonerated the cat from the charge of being a ferocious bird killer. Seventy-four percent of the stomach contents was small rodents, 3.4 percent young rabbits, 19 percent kitchen scraps, and 3.6 percent carrion. An American study supports these findings. Of the 4,771 domestic cat feces examined on a California nature preserve, 21 contained the remains of rabbits; 8, the remains of birds; and 4,742, the remains of rodents—mostly mice.

The "mouse" you offer your cat may be a piece of aluminum foil on a string. Here are some notes on Joan playing mouse with Danny.

Joan rustled the "mouse." Danny sighted it, crouched, and ran speedily toward it in the stalking run. His body was almost flat against the ground; his forelegs made a sharp angle at the elbows and projected above the shoulder blades. His tail was stretched straight out behind, its tip twitching gently. His head was forward, whiskers spread wide, and ears erect and aimed at the toy prey. This is the run-stalk.

The prey lay still. Danny moved forward. Joan jiggled it. He prepared for a pounce by gradually lifting his rear heels off the ground until he was on his toes, his hind paws moving rhythmically up and down, rocking his whole hindquarters. His stretched tail twitched. He sprang, going for the mark not in one leap but in several bounds, keeping low. He struck the prey at ground level—the pounce.

The aluminum foil escaped Danny, and he positioned himself steadily for another pounce by grounding his hind feet securely. Stabilized, he was ready to follow any evasive movement. But now something happened that could not happen in nature. The "mouse" was transformed into a "bird" as Joan lifted the foil into the air.

Cats hunt birds by bending the paw at the wrist and sweeping the arm upwards. If you are sitting on the couch and the cat is under it, it will use this technique to catch you—and your attention. Had there been a way for Joan to dangle the toy below Danny, she would have transformed it into a "fish." The fish-catching paw and arm is a downward scoop with the paw bent like hook and the claws extended. Cats that sit on refrigerators and tops of bookcases "fish" for you when you pass by. I respond to all these overly realistic hunting games with a spit-growl. Sometimes it works, but not always. Cats love hunting games and practically nothing discourages them.

Sometimes more serious motives overwhelm the let's-pretend quality. My friend Gretchen Chinnock learned that from a tabby cat named Scruffy. He called on her every morning, asked to come in through the window, and slept on the couch. But after her daughter visited with her cat, Scruffy sniffed the room, the closet, and "his" couch, then stared at Gretchen and slipped under the chair where she was accustomed to read the morning paper. An hour or so later, having forgotten all about him, she sat down for her morning read. A paw shot out and up from under the chair and nabbed her, bird style.

As Danny's play bird rose into the air, he swatted, scooping upwards with unsheathed claws and spread toes. One claw snagged the foil. He held it, foreleg extended. Were it a bird, it would not get away.

You would think that when a cat discovered that this entrancingly moving object was only string and foil, devoid of warmth, fur, feathers, or scents, it would lose interest. But Danny, like many other cats, went on with the hunt, for he was as stimulated by the game as he would have been on a real hunt. He was exuberant. He flopped to his side, and his right foreleg seemed to come out of his shoulder as he reached for the prey. This movement said the aluminum foil was a mouse. Joan responded by making it act like one, keeping it as still as a mouse when a cat is around. Danny reached with the mouse scoop he uses to catch mice. Then, stretching his

THE CAT'S HUNTING MOVEMENTS

Mousing

Fishing

Bugging

Birding

foreleg from the shoulder, he lifted his paw, and prepared to smash down on the victim from above.

Joan gave the prey a hard jerk, and it flew past Danny's head and got away like a bird. Danny looked dumbfounded. His wide eyes and open mouth said so. Nothing is supposed to get away from *him*, despite the fact that it often does in games. His genes were stronger than his memory. Cats expect to be successful and are incredulous when they are not. The prey returned, moving like a mouse. Danny pounced and bit. That successful denouement ended the game.

A variety of cat toys and play techniques will evoke a variety of cat responses, adding to your and your cat's pleasure in games. You can drum up a search by rustling paper and scratching the floor with your fingernails. I squeak like a mouse by kissing the back of my hand and squeezing air through my teeth. Trinket, upon hearing these sounds, would come on the search from the upstairs bedroom down to the kitchen and meow in protest when she found only me.

A fake fur-covered or plush ball evokes the killing bite, given from the top, as though to the nape of the neck. The toy should be no bigger than about two inches in diameter. Domestic cats can catch any live animal not bigger than themselves, but rarely take on anything larger than a rat or pheasant. Trinket's favorite hunting toys were about the size of a mouse. We also liked to see her strategy for smaller prey, and for this we used a "butterfly"—a small piece of paper attached to a string.

Cats hunt insects, frogs, and toads, not with one paw as with a mouse, but two. When we fluttered the butterfly

toy above Trinket, she would hop, clap her paws together, then take a calculating look, leap, and close. This was not a favorite game, because it is difficult for cats to jump up and catch flying objects.

Rarely did she play rat hunt with me, a game that is the same as mouse hunt but with a larger object. The size of the "rat" turned her off. Cats do hunt rats, but with some reluctance, since these animals are vicious fighters and often turn and attack. For a cat to be attacked by the prey is not in its game plan at all, and when this happens, it goes into the anxiety dance—leaping backward, hind legs stretched stiff—then bolts.

However, you can get the flavor of how a rat is killed by using a smallish stuffed animal (one that is no longer wanted) on a string. Just as a cat attacks a rival by rolling onto its back, holding on with its front claws and slashing upward with rear claws, so it attacks a rat by rolling under it and batting it so rapidly and incessantly that it exhausts the beast. From the relatively safe position below the belly, it kills the rat with a bite to the chest or throat. Jerking the "rat" after your cat has a good grip on it will stimulate the belly-raking and throat-biting responses. It is not advisable to let small children try this, because if they get their hands in the way of the action, they will be scratched and bitten too.

Trinket was a ratter when the real thing invaded the house. She worked from nine o'clock one evening until dawn the next morning to catch a rat. Stalking, waiting, and finally driving it into the exposed springs of a swivel desk chair, she held it as if by a paw by never taking her eyes off the beast for one instant. At 5:00 A.M. the rat moved out, so still was Trinket. That was it. She grabbed it, rolled under it, and quickly killed the exhausted animal. She walked off and never came back to eat it. I tossed it in the garbage.

THE REAL THING

Several days after I took notes on Danny's play hunting, he found a live mouse.

For an hour he lay in wait for it, stalked, lay in wait, and then cornered it under the china closet, holding it motionless with his eyes. By not moving, a mouse vanishes from trouble. A cat needs motion to inspire a strike. All predators see motionless things, but not as well as moving ones. It is like someone pointing out a motionless deer in the woods to you. You barely see it, if at all, until it leaps off. Then it not only becomes clear but inspires a reaction. Some shoot, others pause and smile in admiration and awe.

Joan rattled the china closet. The mouse darted out. Danny saw it and pursued, bounding low to the ground. He pounced, slapped it down with a paw, and grabbed it by the nape of the neck—the cat's classic mouse catch. He bit. The bite was fatal.

Dead mouse before him, Danny did something that has puzzled cat watchers for ages. He laid the little corpse down on the floor, walked away, sat down some feet away from it, and proceeded to groom himself. Leyhausen calls this "taking a walk" and believes it is not so much a blasé attitude toward killing as it is a working off of tension. Little John Henry worked off tension under a different stressful circumstance. Attempting to defuse the aggressiveness of the many-times-larger cat to whose home he had been introduced, he would bat at his housemate while burbling fond greetings. Then, rebuffed by the old cat's baleful stare, John Henry would withdraw his paw and groom it avidly.

More puzzling still, and deeply upsetting to many, is the behavior of a cat that does not immediately kill its prey but only stuns or wounds it with a blow of the claws. William walks away from his stunned prey, returns, bats at it and tosses it as though it were nothing more than a toy on a string, leaves again, and repeats the cruel game until, probably by accident, the creature dies. Michael Fox explains this macabre behavior simply: It is a short circuit. Each step in the hunting sequence is triggered in the cat's brain by a stimulus. The stimulus to stalk and pounce is the prey's movement; the stimulus to give the killing bite is hunger. William is, by any standards, a fat cat. Moving mice trigger him to stalk and pounce, but his stomach doesn't trigger him to kill. Relieving tension, he takes a walk, sits down, grooms—and notices the moving mouse. Again he stalks, cuts off the animal's escape by those alternating paw swipes that toss it from side to side,

pounces—and leaves. His normal sequence is short-circuited by his full belly.

Danny tosses even a dead mouse, not because it twitches of its own accord but because, returning, his own pawing animates the corpse and triggers his swiping reflex.

Very often during the walk, prey that has been merely stunned escapes. Trinket invariably caught chipmunks by one claw, which did not kill but sent them into motionless shock. Presuming them dead, she would lay them down and take a walk, only to return and find they had revived and run away to see another day. It will come as a relief to those who can't bear to see suffering to know that a cat's attack releases in its prey a neurotransmitter that blocks pain and anxiety. The chemical, similar to morphine, renders the victim insensible to its predicament. It is alive only in a physiological, not a psychological, sense.

When Danny was stalking the mouse, his whiskers were fully stretched in the direction of the action. When, however, he picked up the dead prey, his whiskers enveloped it as if to protect it from thieves. The whiskers of a cat are organs of touch that bring in spatial information about the close-in environment, such as the size of holes or passageways through brush.

By touching cats' whiskers, and also what are called *sinus hairs* on the upper and lower edges of the lips, scientists have discovered a number of efficient reflexes that aid in hunting. Depending on which whisker, sinus hair, or lip area is touched, a cat will blink, turn the head away, or slam the jaws shut.

I picked up Danny's deserted mouse and examined it. The stab wound was miraculously clean. Only a small drop of blood revealed where this incredible surgeon had severed the spinal cord with a slash of a single canine tooth. Research has shown that the canine teeth of the cat have an automatic pilot. They hit the nape, slide down between two vertebrae, and, using the space within the joint as a guide, glide down to the spinal cord. Once there, nerves at the root of the canine tooth send messages to the jaw muscles. They close with enormous strength and with lightning speed.

I put the mouse down, and Danny clutched it. He carried it swinging between his two front feet, and he himself reeled slightly from side to side to swing it and keep it from hitting his legs. When he had transported it to the threshold of Joan's home office, he dropped his burden. That is as far as the prey of some cats ever goes. William the Fat brings the trophies of his hunts to his first-order home as offerings to the family, much as Belknap brought mouse presents to Trinket and her kittens, but he seldom dines on anything more hearty than the delicacies, such as mouse liver.

Danny plucked some of the mouse's fur, a final nicety before the feast, and licked the mouse's flank to clean off the plucked hair from his rough tongue. Gathering all four feet under himself, he crouched, the favorite eating pose of the domestic cat. He adjusted the mouse in his mouth, and then, using the carnassial teeth in the rear of his mouth as scissors, he cut the prey into small pieces. He swallowed them whole, neatly and without chewing. His paws did not enter into the action at all but remained tucked tidily under him. When the mouse was consumed—ears, toes, tail, and all—he licked his paw, and with it he washed his face, whiskers, and the backs of his ears. Gracefully he arose and walked off to his sunning spot on the windowsill. Slowly he closed his eyes, a smile on his lips.

EXCLAMATION POINTS

Whether active or in repose, cat expressions are emphasized by their eyes, ears, tail, and even their markings. These ex-

clamation points are worth careful observation if you wish
to catch the finer meanings in cat expression.

The coloring of the face, tail, back, and belly of the cat
emphasizes what is being said. White teeth are outlined by
dark lips, and wrinkled noses are seen more clearly by the
gathering of dark hairs in the grooves made by contracting
facial muscles. The light belly, like the dog's, speaks of sub-
missiveness when exposed, not to a leader but to a mate or
rival. Some cats, in addition, have those eyes, or threat spots,
on the backs of the ears with which Parson held off Riley
long enough to gain the top of the couch. Cat expert George
Schaller suggests that the spots are also "Follow-me" signals
that shine out like eyes on a mother cat and guide kittens
through tall grass and shadowy forest. Trinket, who had these
spots, seemed to use them that way. I saw her take her kittens
into the tall grass by the woodpile. They would deviate from
her footsteps, get lost, leap up, possibly see those eyes in that
moment of aerial suspension, and catch up with her. But
perhaps they were zeroing in on her upraised tail.

The splendid cat tail is a semaphore that sends messages
of friendship and warning, as well as "state-of-the cat" announcements. On windowsills and beside hearths sit cats with
tails curled around their bodies announcing their comfort to
everyone who cares to hear. When Trinket was walking about
relaxed, she carried her tail loosely down, slightly out from
her body, the tip curled gently upward—like all cats at ease.

After a slight rise in emotion, caused perhaps by a loved
person moving around in the first-order home, the cat will
express its cheerfulness by raising the tail, softly curved.

The greeting-tail hello with which Danny speaks to Joan
is straight up and not curved at all—the flagpole. He greets
me, however, with a slight reservation, holding his tail like
an upside-down J. That crick on the end means, "I am not
sure of you." Most cats give the J signal to strange people.

They feel friendly toward them, but not straight-up, all-out friendly. Reply to this by holding your hand out for a bout of sniff reading by the cat so that it can learn about your attitude and personality.

Danny tail talked when he had the mouse cornered under the china closet. The tip twitched and quivered to say, "This is my mouse. All other cats and people stand back." Beware that twitching tip; it is a warning. William tried to tell Sara's husband, Marty, not to bother him one evening. The cat was lying before him on the dining room table, twitching his tail. Marty reached out to pet William just as Sara saw the tail and warned him not to touch. Too late, the paw followed the "Don't-bother-me" warning.

While walking, a cat expresses this same message with a crick that begins at the base of the tail and moves upwards to the top, leaving a wake of bristling fur behind. As it reaches the top, every hair is standing out like a bottlebrush to accentuate the "I'm-going-to-swat-you" message.

That bristle tail is also a vivid signal in the Halloween-cat pose, a posture so magnificent that it has become the symbol of courage and defiance. It is best seen when the cat faces a strange dog. It stretches itself up to the full height of the legs and arches the back. The body hairs rise, and at the base of the tail, that crick begins, moves upward, and disappears, leaving the bristling flagpole. This is all offensive talk. If the dog is provoked to come on, defensive pronouncements, all in the same pose, are added. The ears flatten to the head, the mouth opens and exposes the sharp canine teeth, and the head draws in to protect the nape of the neck. The Halloween cat hisses and stands broadside to the enemy to appear bigger and more formidable. "I am ready to kill. I am ready to swat and flee," says this, the most expressive of all animal postures.

Tail emphases are mirrored by facial expressions as a

THE CAT'S TAIL POSITIONS

"All's well."

"I like you, with reservations."

"I like you all out!"

"You make me worried."

"I'm on the defensive."

"You're boss."

"I'm a humble cat."

"That mouse is mine."

"Got it!"

cat shifts from a pleasant mood to an angry one.

The cat face has six readable expressions. Each expression is an honest announcement of what is to come. A good cat-face reader can prepare for a swat, a bite, or a purr by quickly interpreting the facial announcements.

When your cat is simply saying, "I feel affection and want to be caressed," the ears are up and forward, and the head is tilted slightly downward. The pupils are almost round in the center of the eye. The lower lid rises slightly, softening the whole expression. The mouth seems to smile. The cat is prepared to purr if you stroke it or pick it up and hug it.

"Someone is coming," says the cat face with the ears up, eyes wide, pupils narrow, lips and whiskers relaxed. Danny would wear this face when another cat was approaching. As his concern increased, his ears would twist back until their openings faced to the side, and his pupils would dilate.

Unsure of who this "someone" was, he would shift to the offensive-defensive face. His head would lower as he stared. His ears would twist forward from their very bases, as if to pick up even the rustle of a whisker. His pupils would dilate wider. The meaning is ambiguous: "I might run. I might attack."

Step out of reach and watch for any further deterioration of mood once a cat states its uncertainty, for if it shifts toward the defensive-threat face, the cat is warning you of a swat and perhaps a bite that will draw blood.

As Danny progresses toward a mean mood, his ears flatten, his pupils dilate yet further, and his mouth opens, momentarily displaying his lower canines. Then the mouth closes, and the ears rotate forward but remain flattened. Finally, the defensive-threat face: Ears are rotated back now and so flattened that they are not visible from the front, the mouth is wide open, showing all four canines and the tongue, and Danny is spitting. His eyes become black as the pupils dilate completely. In a moment he will make good his threat to attack.

The cat's eyes, so expressively large for its head, are indices of its feelings. Research at the University of Chicago psychology department indicates that cat pupils, those vertical slits that expand in darkness and contract in light, also respond to the thoughts and feelings of the cat. The same is true of humans. Tests reveal that the pupils of our eyes dilate when gazing at a lover, when about to fight, and even when, of several available beverages, we sip the one we prefer. Our dilations are not, however, dramatically large. A cat's pupils dilate four or five times their former size when it is hungry and sees its well-supplied feeding dish. They also dilate when it sees photographs of a strange cat or of its favorite people.

We tend to think that animals cannot recognize objects in photographs, but a cat-sitter for a tabby named Rachel, owned by two Yale professors, told them when they returned from vacation that Rachel had sat on the dressing table staring at the family photograph for hours each day.

Cat eyes shine at night, throwing off colors that vary from yellow-green or blue-green to red. In the Middle Ages witch-hunters believed that the shine came from little windows that opened on the fires of hell, an apt description of the eerie flashing lights in the cat's eyes when the beam from headlight or flashlight strikes them in the dark.

The shine is actually a reflection from a mirror, a layer of cells of crystalline substance in the cat's eye. With this arrangement an image is "twice seen," once as light hits the retina on its way in, and again as it is bounced back through the retina from the reflective layer behind it. The double exposure helps the cat make the best possible use of available light under low-light conditions, such as when it is hunting at night.

That aloof look of the cat has a scientific explanation. We bring objects into sharp focus on a cluster of cells in the center of our eye called the *fovea*. Cats do not have this central point. They see primarily out of the periphery, which requires no focusing of the pupils. The impression given is of looking without looking, or of dreaming of visions. Many people find the far-off gaze cold and disturbing.

When a cat does stare at something for a long time, it either fears it or has designs on it. With the stare it is taking aim for the death bite. That is why cats themselves do not like to be stared at. Paul Leyhausen noted that when one of his cats was creeping up on its prey and realized another cat was watching, it instantly straightened up and lost interest in the pursuit.

Cats stare at prey and rival cats, but they do not look long into the eyes of lovers and mates as we do. Trinket never once looked for more than a second or two at Belknap, keeping those long looks for mice and rats.

She did not like her kittens to stare at her either. If one kept its eyes on her while she was coming toward it, she stopped, sat down, and looked away. Lion tamers, however, make use of the direct stare to control their animals. According to Paul Leyhausen, it works because the trainer's stare maintains his superior rank.

You, too, can talk to your cat with your eyes, but beware. It is not at all like looking into the eyes of your dog to

THE CAT'S ANGRY FACES

During an aggressive encounter the pupils of the eye, the angle of the ears, and the raising of the fur are clues to what the cat is feeling.

"All's well."	*"I'm alarmed."*	*"I'm going to attack."*
"But maybe I won't."	*"I warn you . . ."*	*". . . I'll swat!"*
"I warn you, I'll bite."	*"Keep your distance . . ."*	*" . . .or else!!"*

convey love and affection. I kept trying to make friends with Freud, the psychiatrist's cat. One evening I was observing him as he sat atop the couch. My look, it seemed to me, was barely a stare, but before I could say, "Nice kitty," he was off the couch and speeding toward me like a launched jet. He clamped his teeth on my wrist.

On the other hand, a cat feels free to stare at you, and when it does, it usually wants something—food, the chair you are sitting on, your attention and affection.

Unbeknownst to many, people are talking to their cat when they read or write. By staring at a book or letter for a long time, we are announcing to the cat that we have something very interesting lined up. To a cat's way of thinking, we are inviting it to come and sit upon this fascinating "place" within its rightful environment. The cat obliges and sits down, only to be confused when it is picked up and dropped to the floor.

A better way to get rid of the cat on your paperwork is to tell it to sit somewhere else by staring at another book or piece of paper. Of course, you don't get much accomplished this way, for cats take their time in moving to this marching order. Furthermore, when you go back to your work or resume reading your book, you are telling the cat to come back again. It usually obeys. This can go on for hours. Cats have lots of time.

My friend Peg Bradfield, an illustrator, solved this problem once and for all. She had a tom named Jenkins who sat on every sketch as she worked on it. She tried to tell him to go elsewhere by staring at pillows and corners of her studio. He heeded, but only briefly.

One night she was working late to make a morning deadline when Jenkins, at her invitation in his view, jumped onto her drawing board. She did not have time to stare at another piece of paper, and desperation drove her to invention. She went into the kitchen, gathered every brown paper bag she could find, buffeted them open, and set them all over her studio floor. Cats *have* to explore caves. In the human environment caves are usually boxes and paper bags, and for many hours Jenkins went in and out of the caverns seeking whatever cats seek in such places. Peg worked peacefully, and just before sunup she put the last brushstroke on her illustration and arose. Jenkins was tumbling inside the last bag; but Peg's work was done.

Paper bags are the ultimate in polite, genteel communication with a cat. You can hiss, meow, even stare, arch your back, show your teeth, to no avail. But give your cat a paper bag and he bows to your wishes. In he goes—and gets lost.

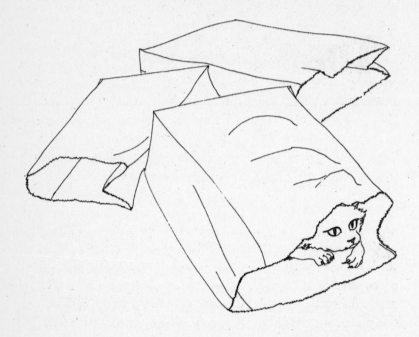

Closer Than We Thought

At a barbecue in the suburbs of Athens, Georgia, I found myself seated on a spacious wooden deck among a group of psychologists and anthropologists, professors and their graduate students. As the night crossed over into morning, the philosopher in each emerged and the truth of yesterday became today's error.

We were discussing animal behavior as a route toward understanding nonhuman communication, and the conversation had been meandering like an old river.

"The first thing we have to do," said an authoritative voice to my left, "is to settle what the difference is between man and the animals so that we know who we are and who they are."

I searched my memory, recalling that when I was in college the word was that the difference between man and beast was our ability to make and use tools. We throw stones, spear food on forks, and carry things in jars and baskets. These achievements, experts believed then, were unique to *Homo sapiens,* and textbooks referred to our species as the *tool user.* That was the late 1930s and early 1940s.

I certainly was not going to mention this long-disproved notion to the esteemed researchers around me, some of whom had just heard the latest in nonhuman tool use from chimpanzee watcher Jane Goodall. While traveling in Serengeti National Park in northern Tanzania, she and her husband, Hugo van Lawick, brought their car to a sudden halt in an open savanna where two Egyptian vultures—white birds with golden cheeks and about the size of ravens—were standing before an ostrich egg. One of the birds had a stone in its beak. It threw back its head, flipped its neck forward, and hurled the stone. It struck the huge thick-shelled egg with a thud. The vulture walked up to the egg, saw that it had not broken, and, doing some obvious thinking, picked up the stone for another try. The next pitch missed the egg entirely, but with the third effort the shell cracked, and it took only a few more hurls to open it.

Sea otters also use stones as hammers. They collect large hard-shelled abalones in their teeth during dives to the sea bottom, then each picks up a stone with its forepaws. Surfacing, the otters roll onto their backs, place the abalones on their bellies, and, clasping a stone in both front feet, smash the shells open.

One of the Galápagos Islands finches uses a cactus spine or a sharp twig as a fork. First, it tests the tool's strength by pressing it against a limb. If it breaks, it seeks a stronger one. Then the bird transfers it to a foot while it uses its beak to drill into the wood of a decaying tree. When an insect is found, the finch takes the spine in its beak again and guides it into the hole. With precision it spears the insect and pulls it out. Shifting the spine to its foot, the bird then eats its meal from the pick.

Jane Goodall was the first to report that at least some animals—the chimpanzees she was observing at Gombe Game Preserve—make the tools they use. To get drinking water trapped in tree cavities, chimpanzees crumple leaves to make a sponge. They "fish" for termites with a probe they fashion by carefully stripping the leaves from a slender branch. The probe is stuck into the termite corridor. Considering themselves invaded, the termites grab the foreign intruder in their jaws and hang on while the chimp pulls them out and eats them like shish kebab.

Impressive as these technologies are, it could be argued that they are instinctive, programmed behavior not comparable to the thoughtful way even a toddler might use a stone one time to crush a peanut, another time to scratch a table, and still another to bang against a pot. That's what I had thought, until Crowbar, our pet crow, taught me a lesson.

Crowbar, who enjoyed playing with my children, was in the sandbox with them one morning. Presently my daughter came running to tell me she did not want to play with Crowbar anymore because he did not play fair. He took all the toys and hoarded them in the crotches of the apple tree. I suggested she slide down the slide.

"Crows can't slide," I explained of my plot to foil the bird. "The bottoms of their feet are horny to keep them from slipping off tree limbs. Crowbar will stick at the top."

Fifteen minutes later I looked out to see my daughter and son sliding down the slide and Crowbar at the top—stuck. He was forced to hop down. I felt smug about having outwitted a crow.

A moment later, Crowbar was back in the sandbox. There he picked up a plastic coffee-can lid, flew with it to the top of the slide, put it down, stepped in it, and—zoom.

The young woman sitting next to me at the barbecue apparently had been mentally going over similar territory. Perhaps, she wondered aloud, an individual animal's failure to pass creative invention along to others marks the boundary between human and nonhuman. No sooner were the words out of her mouth than she retracted them. She had remembered the macaques that have been protected for generations at the Monkey Research Center, Takasakiyama, Japan. For years the monkeys had accepted wheat, soybeans, and sweet potatoes tossed on the ground to supplement the foods they could forage for themselves. These treats, though eagerly sought, were unpleasantly gritty.

In a moment of thoughtful inspiration, a young female monkey scooped up a handful of food and ran to the stream. Seating herself beside a pool, she dumped her sandy ration into the water. The dirt sank to the bottom, the food floated to the surface, and she scooped up the clean morsels and ate them grit-free.

Her mother and siblings observed, understood what she was doing, and learned to wash grain, too.

Ultimately, the food-washing invention was taken up by the younger set. Conservative elders never did go for the new fad, but by the following generation, most had adopted food washing. It had become a tradition.

If that was not sufficiently startling—primates are certainly smart, after all—the spread of an invention among a group of birds in England was enough to make the hair stand on end.

Blue tits, little birds like our chickadees, learned to flip the lids off milk bottles and sip cream during World War II in the village of Swathling, England. The lid-flipping technique spread from a few birds to almost the entire town population of tits and, a year later, to populations in towns ten miles away. The milk industry answered complaints by urging customers to put stones on their porches to be placed on top of the bottles by the milk deliverers. The stones were put out, but customers found them beside, not on top of, the bottles in the morning. More calls to the milk company. Officials insisted the deliverers had put the stones on the bottles. One suspicious housewife got up before dawn and peeked out from behind the blind to see if this were the case. It was true. The deliverer had dutifully placed a stone on each bottle. She was perplexed. Then came the blue tits. Without hesitation they alighted on the stones and pecked at their edges until they shifted over and toppled to the ground. With a whack the pretty blue-and-gold birds flipped the cardboard lids and sipped cream.

The next ploy was to cover the bottles with towels. This halted the assault on the cream for several days, and then towels were found cast aside, and cream sipping resumed. A check at dawn revealed that birds in groups of three or four each took a corner of the towel, lifted it off the bottles while flying, and dropped it; then they flitted back to the bottles, flipped the lids, and sipped.

Diabolically, the milk deliverers placed the morning's delivery in a box open on one side, but barely taller than a milk bottle so that there was no clearance for the birds. This briefly foiled the blue tits, which were now accustomed to matching their wits with humans'.

But before long the blue tits, now on their mental toes, simply flew into the open-backed milk trucks while the milkmen shoved bottles into the box on the stoop, and sipped cream there.

My mind drifted on the wings of birds as the balmy night drew on and the conversation flowed—I was remembering a chicken.

Her name was Helen, and she belonged to my childhood

friend Virginia. She was one of those Easter gifts who grew from a cute fuzzy plaything into a serious personality. Helen was much more than a hen. She not only followed my friend but called her to meals by clucking furiously if Virginia did not hear her mother's dinner call. She conveniently laid an egg a day on a towel in the corner near the kitchen stove. She made a hobby of carrying pebbles from one bowl to another, for no apparent reason but that it amused everyone, not least herself. When Virginia and I played jump rope, Helen flew back and forth over the low swinging rope, clucking and carrying on in her "Look-what-I-did" egg-laying voice.

Then there was Sam. I would never have believed in Sam had I not met a professional naturalist who knew him and Peter, a boy of ten, and reported her observations to me. Sam was Peter's box turtle.

"Do you love me, Sam?" the boy asked as he gently held him against his throat beneath his chin. Slowly Sam opened his box, slowly extended his head and neck, and moved them gently back and forth against Peter's throat.

"He's saying 'I love you,' " Peter explained.

"Tell me you love me good," he insisted and tipped his chin against Sam. The turtle stroked Peter again.

"Let's go for a walk, Sam," Peter said, and slowly Sam pulled into his shell. Peter put him in his pocket and strode out the door and down the path.

I thought of all manner of scientific explanations for Sam's behavior: that the warmth of the boy's skin had made the turtle stretch his neck; that the pressure on his shell had provoked him to—something. But Peter's mother reported this:

"Sam sleeps with Peter—right on his chest."

"Of course Peter puts him there?"

"Oh, no. Sam climbs up the tumbled blankets when

Peter is asleep, walks onto his chest, and stops. He pulls his head and neck into his box. I presume he's sleeping too. He's very quiet."

Could it be that animals so different from ourselves can be brought out of their faraway worlds into communication with humans?

"Well, one thing is certain," a voice interrupted my musings. "We can't say that the difference between man and nonhuman animals is that only we use language."

"That's still controversial," said a graduate student in psychology whose mentor was one of the firm believers that animals cannot use language.

Most linguists concur that two criteria must be met for a system of communication to constitute a language. One is that the words or signs be symbols for something and recognized as such by the user. That may or may not be a reasonable demand. Jean Piaget, the Swiss psychologist who did more to unravel the thought processes of children than perhaps anyone, discovered that to a three-year-old, words are the objects they stand for. They use symbols without knowing that they do.

The other criterion for a communication system to be a language is that the symbols be combinable with one another to form novel phrases or sentences that are nonetheless understandable by others. Any three-year-old can do that.

Research efforts to resolve the question of whether or not animals could use language foundered for a while on the fact that even our closest relative, the chimpanzee, hasn't the vocal apparatus to speak. Chimps raised like babies within a human family had learned to grunt a few words like "cup" or "milk," but no more.

Then, in the late 1960s, psychologists began to circumvent that obstacle by using nonvocal languages. David Premack of the University of California at Santa Barbara used plastic symbols of different shapes to represent words. He claimed that chimp Sarah learned some 130 words and phrases with this technique, but admitted that she had created nothing new to say.

Psychologists Allen and Beatrice Gardner of the University of Nevada fueled the debate when they taught the chimp Washoe to communicate with humans in American Sign Language (Ameslan), a gestural language used by the deaf. Washoe astounded scientist and layman alike not only by learning 125 signs but by inventing a novel phrase of her own. One day, seeing a swan swimming on a lake, but not knowing the sign for it, Washoe excitedly signed out "water bird."

Skeptics Dr. Duane Rumbaugh of Georgia State University and his wife, Susan Savage Rumbaugh, suggested that the people who were teaching the chimps these novel nonvocal languages were so involved with the animals that they were suffering from the Clever Hans effect. Clever Hans, a horse who lived around the turn of the century, was credited for a time with being able to solve arithmetic problems. When shown an addition or subtraction problem written on a blackboard, he would stamp out the correct answer with his hoof. Close study showed that Clever Hans did not know the answers. Instead he was picking up subtle clues from his trainer, who was unaware himself of what he was doing, that told the horse when to start and when to stop stamping.

This made skeptics of almost all animal behaviorists for the next forty years.

To offset the possibility that researchers were unconsciously cueing their students, Rumbaugh invented a language based on ancient Chinese, dubbed it *Yerkish,* reduced the words to lexigrams, or symbols, and programmed them into a computer at the Yerkes Primate Research Center in Atlanta.

A special keyboard using the Yerkish lexigrams was de-

signed, and the computer was connected to various appurtenances, such as a vending machine and a movie projector. In
order to obtain, say, a candy, the chimp would have to ask
for it in a certain way: "Please, machine, give [name of chimp]
candy." Each word was a symbol over a button, and correctly
stated requests were answered automatically. A bright young
chimp named Lana was domiciled in a playroom fitted to a
chimp's taste with swings, windows, ledges—and the computer. After a few demonstrations, Lana was adroitly pushing
the correct lexigrams in the correct syntax to obtain all her
needs: water, food, candy, movies of chimps. By pushing the
right buttons she could call Tim, a graduate student and her
human friend, to come play with her and relieve her boredom
with the machine.

Lana toppled mankind's superiority complex when she
not only learned which buttons to push to get what she wanted
but forced her human friends to create new lexigrams for
items that had not originally been programmed into the machine. One day she taught Tim to tickle her, a favorite chimpanzee pleasure, and then got the idea across to put the word
"tickle" on the machine. After that, she could push the buttons to say, "Please, Tim, come tickle Lana." Over the years
she learned 125 word-symbols, developed counting skills,
and compared piles of objects to say which had the greater
number.

"Twenty years ago," said Rumbaugh in the winter of
1984, "if you had told me that apes could learn words in a
meaningful way, I and other scientists would have said, 'That's
impossible.' Now that's no longer a question. The answer is
yes, they do."

The naysaying graduate student was upholding the opposition. He referred to the work of psychologist Herbert
Terrace of Columbia University and his little chimp Nim (full

name Nim Chimpsky, a play on the name of linguist Noam Chomsky of M.I.T., a proponent of the idea that language ability is biologically unique to humans). Terrace and his students put Nim through forty-four months of intensive sign-language drill while treating him much as they would a child. He learned aptly, signing "dirty" when he wanted to use the potty or "drink" when he spotted someone sipping from a thermos. Nim, said Terrace, nonetheless did not master even the rudiments of grammar or sentence construction. Unlike children, his speech did not grow in complexity, nor did it show much spontaneity. Eighty-eight percent of the time, he "talked" only in response to questions from his teachers. Terrace studied the tapes of other apes and concluded, "The closer I looked, the more I regarded the many reported instances of language as elaborate tricks (by the apes) for obtaining rewards."

If so, an ape had certainly fooled me. I had visited the famous Lana in the company of Dr. Rumbaugh to see this wunderkind for myself. As we approached the two-way glass side of her playroom, the alert chimp turned, saw me with her friend, and began to show off. She swung down to her machine, which glowed with symbols for some fifty words at that time, and smiled a toothy chimpanzee smile. The symbols on the keyboard had translations behind the scenes for the professors and assistants, who could not remember them all.

Glancing at me once again, she began typing, moving her hands so rapidly that I could barely follow the sequence of buttons she pushed.

"Please, machine." She pushed two of the lexigrams. "Give Lana M & M's." Three more buttons were pushed. Tim, who had been taking notes behind a one-way window where Lana couldn't see him, suddenly stood up. Lana was looking at the "water" button. She wanted M & M's *and* water. She needed a new word. She needed "and" right then and there to circumvent the long procedure of pushing two full sentences of lexigrams.

"That's when the machine seems frustrating," Tim said to me later. "I can't give her the new word she wants fast enough. She thinks faster than we can work."

"I think it's a matter of cultivating a process that's inherent in chimps," Dr. Rumbaugh explained to me. "They can symbolize. They can learn; absolutely they can learn."

Dr. Rumbaugh knows, as every pet owner knows, that the more you talk to an animal, whether in its language or ours, the smarter and more aware it becomes.

"Language changes and enhances chimps' lives," he said. "The language-smart chimps are much more reflective and communicative. They interrelate with humans differently and more effectively and are more clever in learning and solving problems. Even their demeanor is changed. They are less destructive and much more careful in their interacting with people."

There is not an animal owner who would not agree. The cats, dogs, birds, and horses—even wild creatures that have been brought into a dialogue with humans—seem to grow more clever, considerate, and aware. They are more careful of us.

Or is it the other way around? It seemed to me, watching Lana spell out her wishes to "machine," that opening up an avenue of communication between our two separate species had increased our awareness, sensitivity, and intelligence as much as it had the chimps'. Perhaps we are becoming clever enough to see just how clever they have always been.

As I left the incredible Lana to manipulate her human friends with her machine, Tim accompanied me.

"At long last," he said enthusiastically, "we are beginning to talk to the animals. Soon I will be able to ask Lana the sixty-four-dollar question."

"And what is that?" I asked.

"What do you think of people?"

That question may have been answered by Koko, a hulking female gorilla taught sign language by Francine Patterson, a psychologist at Stanford University.

Koko has made her human companions aware not only that her breed is bright, but that it shares devious abilities commonly held to be unique to people.

Koko can lie, argue, and insult.

Writes Patterson:

At six o'clock on a spring evening, I went to the trailer where Koko lives to put her to bed. I was greeted by Cathy Ransom, one of my assistants, who told me she and Koko had been arguing. The dispute began when Koko was shown a poster of herself. Using hands and fingers, Cathy had asked Koko, "What's this?"

"Gorilla," signed Koko.

"Who gorilla?" asked Cathy.

"Bird," responded bratty Koko, and things went downhill from there.

"You bird?" asked Cathy.

"You," countered Koko.

"Not me. You are bird," rejoined Cathy, mindful that "bird" can be an insult in Koko's lexicon.

"Me gorilla," asserted Koko.

"Who bird?" asked Cathy.

"You nut," signed Koko.

"You nut, not me," Cathy replied.

Finally, Koko gave up. Plaintively she signed, "Damn, me good," and walked away.

"What makes all this awesome," continues Patterson, "is that Koko, by all accepted concepts of animal and human nature, should not be able to do any of this. Traditionally, such behavior has been considered uniquely human; yet here is a language-using gorilla."

Koko can get into contrary moods, once considered the prerogative of humans. Patterson can almost program her actions when she is in such a mood. When she was breaking plastic spoons, an assistant signed, "Good, break them," and instantly Koko stopped breaking them and started kissing them. She knows she is misbehaving on these occasions and once described herself as a "stubborn devil."

Koko has a rich collection of insults that she has invented—"rotten stink" and "dirty toilet," as well as "bird" and "nut." These she applies to people whom she is not getting along with. During a fit of pique she referred to Patterson, whom she calls Penny, as "Penny toilet dirty devil"—a real achievement in creativity in any language.

Koko creates not only novel phrases and meanings but new symbols. She is terrified of alligators, although she has never seen a real one, just toothy facsimiles. For signing about them, she has invented her own word by snapping the two palms together in an imitation of an alligator's jaws closing. "Large alligator" is a big movement with her arms; "little alligator" is a tiny movement with her fingers.

Koko can refer to events removed in time and space, a sophisticated characteristic of human language known to linguists as *displacement*.

Patterson: "What did you do to Penny?"

Koko: "Bite." (The bite, which had occurred three days earlier, had been called a scratch by Koko at the time.)

Patterson: "You admit it?"
Koko: "Sorry bite scratch."
Patterson: "Why bite?"
Koko: "Because mad."
Patterson: "Why mad?"
Koko: "Don't know."

But was Koko really ignorant of her motive? A wonderful thing about language is that it can be used to deceive as well as inform, to evade as well as confront.

It was during a confrontation with a reporter that Koko might indirectly have answered the question, What do you think of people? The reporter wanted to know whether Koko, who had been raised among people her whole life, thought of herself as a fellow human. Translating, Patterson signed: "Are you an animal or a person?" Instantly came Koko's response: "Fine animal gorilla."

Until recently animal-speech teachers thought language had to be taught by humans to each individual primate and could not be passed on to other members of the species.

Again the animals proved us wrong. All the chimpanzees that learned sign and symbol language are now teaching their knowledge to offspring and to untutored adult chimps. All are conversing.

The conversation at the barbecue heated into an argument as to whether or not the chimps and Koko know what they are saying, and promptly stalemated. The question pivots on the word "know," for if Koko knows she is a "fine animal gorilla," then she is conscious, aware of herself and of her thoughts. Consciousness, particularly self-consciousness, has become the last bastion for those who would protect our uniqueness among animals.

All other differences have scattered like duckpins under strike after strike of facts.

Our esthetic sense?

The male bowerbird is an artist. With a sense of design he skillfully decorates his love arbor with colorful petals, berries, and "found" objects to please the critic—the female. Certain colors are more favored than others, and each ornament is placed to emphasize its position within an overall design. Moreover, one species of this bird, the regent bowerbird, paints with a brush and pigment. He mixes earth colors, plant pigments, and charcoal with saliva, dips a wadded leaf or piece of bark in the paint, and daubs the walls of the bower he has built. The results are murals of passionate gray-blue or green.

Our ability to plan, to imagine a future event?

The alpha male wolf can figure out a strategy for attacking prey and, what is more, communicate the plan to his hunters.

Wage war? Commit murder?

There are those who find our violence and inhumanity toward man the blatant difference between us and the animals. But chimps in the Gombe Game Preserve wage war on neighboring groups that infringe on their territory, and they kill members of their own group for motives no easier to discern than "senseless" human murders.

"Our knowledge of death," a young woman had concluded earlier in the evening.

"No," I spoke up.

I had heard a Pulitzer Prize–winning scientist speak to this difference one night in Arizona, stating that the knowledge of death was the important difference between man and beast.

But had he ever seen a crow find a dead companion and bell out the death knell? Had he ever seen a crow die of strychnine-poisoned grain and then heard the flock mournfully announce the death? And did the speaker know that the crows, seeing such a disaster, learn which corn is poisoned and tell their offspring and friends?

The question of consciousness is less easily laid to rest. Crows may fear poison as wolves fear hunters, and both may connect such dangers to the sense of loss death arouses in humans too. But do they think, I, too, will die? Or do even uncannily "human" responses like Koko's self-identification as a "fine animal gorilla" represent merely mechanical learning? She might, after all, have been showing no more comprehension of her words than a child who has been taught to recite the alphabet, but who is unaware of what the letters stand for or that they can be spelled into meanings.

The discussion on that suburban deck ended around three o'clock when the moon was setting behind the pines. As we arose to leave, I felt unsatisfied. After hours of hashing and rehashing we had not concluded anything. I approached our host, the most venerable and renowned member of that late-night group of philosophers.

"So what does it all mean?" I asked.

"That we are closer to the animals than we think," came the answer.

As I stepped down from the deck, I felt I was stepping down from a tower we had mistakenly built to keep us above all other animals. I felt my kinship with the singing bird, the howling wolf, the blowing horse, and the head-bumping cat. I could see myself in them and was amused as well as impressed. I went to my room thinking of old Will Cramer. It had seemed to me, when I began to research the how-to of talking to animals, that the Will Cramers of this world would supply the magic—the intuition that, as he had told me, was "beyond words"—and that scientists would supply the hard facts. Now I realized that was not quite the case. For all their careful study, researchers eventually come face-to-face with communication that is beyond words, and for all their innocence, gifted laymen eventually uncover undeniable facts.

PET CARE

__THE TOTAL DOG BOOK__ *(N31-428, $4.95, U.S.A.)*
by Louis L. Vine, D.V.M. *(N31-429, $5.95, Canada)*

This book goes into every aspect of every problem and challenge you can encounter with your pet, reveals the latest knowledge and newest developments in the field of dog care, and gives practical advice on how to be the best possible master to the most important dog in your life.

"The finest, most authoritative and up-to-date book on dog care . . . a must for every dog owner!"—Cecily R. Collins, breeder, exhibitor

__THE COMMON SENSE BOOK OF
COMPLETE CAT CARE__ *(N31-167, $3.95, U.S.A.)*
by Louis L. Vine, D.V.M. *(N31-168, $4.95, Canada)*

If you love your cat, you will love this book. This practicing veterinarian (who is also an award-winning writer) tells you all you need to know to give the best care and most understanding to your cat from the time you pick your pet through all the years of your lives together.

WARNER BOOKS
P.O. Box 690
New York, N.Y. 10019

Please send me the books I have checked. I enclose a check or money order (not cash), plus 50¢ per order and 50¢ per copy to cover postage and handling.* (Allow 4 weeks for delivery.)

_____ Please send me your free mail order catalog. (If ordering only the catalog, include a large self-addressed, stamped envelope.)

Name _____

Address _____

City _____

State _____ Zip _____

*N.Y. State and California residents add applicable sales tax.   124